Breaking the Mold of Classroom Management

What Educators Should Know and Do to Enable Student Success

Andrea Honigsfeld and Audrey Cohan

ROWMAN & LITTLEFIELD EDUCATION
A division of
ROWMAN & LITTLEFIELD
Lanham • Boulder • New York • Toronto • Plymouth, UK

Published by Rowman & Littlefield Education
A division of Rowman & Littlefield
4501 Forbes Boulevard, Suite 200, Lanham, Maryland 20706
www.rowman.com

10 Thornbury Road, Plymouth PL6 7PP, United Kingdom

British Library Cataloguing in Publication Information Available

Library of Congress Cataloging-in-Publication Data

Andrea Honigsfeld and Audrey Cohan
Breaking the Mold of Classroom Management : What Educators Should Know and Do to Enable Student Success / edited by Andrea Honigsfeld and Audrey Cohan.
p. cm.
Includes bibliographical references.
ISBN 978-1-4758-0347-1 (cloth : alk. paper) -- ISBN 978-1-4758-0348-8 (pbk. : alk. paper) -- ISBN 978-1-4758-0349-5 (electronic)
1. Linguistic minorities--Education. 2. Children of minorities--Education. 3. Multicultural education. 4. Language and culture. I. Honigsfeld, Andrea, 1965- II. Cohan, Audrey.
LC3731.B655 2012
371.829--dc23

2011050653

Printed in the United States of America

Also by Andrea Honigsfeld and Audrey Cohan

Breaking the Mold of Education: Innovative and Successful Practices for Student
Engagement, Empowerment, and Motivation
(R&L Education, 2013)

Breaking the Mold of Education for Culturally and Linguistically Diverse Students
(R&L Education, 2012)

Breaking the Mold of Preservice and Inservice Teacher Education: Innovative and
Successful Practices for the Twenty-first Century
(R&L Education, 2011)

Breaking the Mold of School Instruction and Organization: Innovative and Successful
Practices for the Twenty-First Century
(R&L Education, 2010)

Differentiating Instruction for At-Risk Students: What to Do and How to Do It
(R&L Education, 2009)

We dedicate this book to educators who successfully overcome the challenges of classroom management every day. We will never forget the inspiring and innovative stories teachers have shared with us about creating safe, nurturing, and academically engaging learning environments.

A very special personal acknowledgment goes to our families: Howard, Benjamin, Jacob, and Noah Honigsfeld; Barry, Jeffrey, Lauren, and Matthew Cohan, as well as Susan and Ed Thomas. You are the only ones who truly know how much time and effort went into the *Breaking the Mold* series. Thank you!

Contents

Foreword

Julia G. Thompson

It is a disturbing statistic: almost half of the new teachers who will begin their careers this school year will resign their positions and leave education within five years. One of the significant factors contributing to this profoundly disturbing trend is the incredibly complex and puzzling issue of classroom management. Although many teachers choose a career in education with idealistic dreams of making a difference, the harsh and sometimes chaotic realities of managing a classroom can make those dreams impossible to achieve.

As the author of a book on classroom management, *Discipline Survival Guide for the Secondary Teacher*, I have spent much effort trying to stem the tide of discouraged teachers leaving our profession. As a practicing classroom teacher, I also find myself looking for the best ways to make sure that the students in my classroom are interested, eager, and engaged. I, too, want to create a well-managed classroom environment where success and high achievement are the order of the day.

Breaking the Mold of Classroom Management: What Educators Should Know and Do to Enable Student Success is timely and important. In this remarkable book, the editors, Andrea Honigsfeld and Audrey Cohan, have collected sage advice from some of the best-known and notable educators of our time. The wisdom offered by these distinguished experts provides workable solutions to many of the classroom management challenges that confront today's teachers.

The thought-provoking ideas you will read about here are pragmatic, based on solid classroom research, and, most importantly, inspiring. I wish that I had been able to read this book when I was a beginning teacher, and I am glad that I can read it now.

The effects of centuries of ineffective management practices linger in many classrooms even as you read this. All too often teachers turn to punishment or threats of punishment to attempt to control students even though common sense proves that those toxic practices are clearly not working. Adding to the problem caused by the effects of those harmful practices is a disheartening modern bane—the global economic upheavals that permeate the social fabric of our lives.

Today's increasingly diverse classrooms are filled with overwhelmed teachers struggling to help students with wildly varying readiness levels because their home languages are different from what they are expected to speak at school, their social and academic maturity levels may not be developed fully, or other factors such as inadequate home or cultural support necessary for academic success.

The distinguished contributors to *Breaking the Mold of Classroom Management: What Educators Should Know and Do to Enable Student Success* offer a wealth of evidence-based solutions to overcome these negative influences. First of all, each of the essays is a gem of judicious and useful advice. The topics are broad-ranging; the information you will find here covers the real issues that confront teachers every day such as how to help reluctant learners, dealing with students in a positive and encouraging way, or how to manage a differentiated classroom.

Finally, in this volume, you will discover a common thread of respect for the dignity of students that resonates on every page. You will discover not just innovative recommendations that are satisfyingly grounded in the realities of modern classrooms but also solutions with immediate classroom applications.

It is my hope that as you read through the inspiring, classroom-tested information in this book, you will have the knowledge and confidence to be able to make deliberate and effective choices regarding the management of your classroom. You will be able to use the innovative tools you will find here to create the classroom you want for yourself and your students and fulfill the dreams you had when you first chose a career in education.

—Julia G. Thompson

Acknowledgments

We would like to extend our gratitude to the authors who generously contributed a chapter to this volume and shared their extensive knowledge and empowering message about classroom management with us and our readers. We would also like to thank our friends and colleagues at Molloy College, Rockville Centre, New York and beyond, who have supported us through multiple research and publication projects, and cheered us on as we have completed the five-part *Breaking the Mold* series.

A special thank you goes to our graduate research assistants, Marcella Amenta and Taylor Volpe, whose organizational skills are greatly appreciated.

This project would not have been possible without the support of Dr. Tom Koerner, Chris Basso, Carlie Wall and the hard-working staff of Rowman and Littlefield Publishing. Thank you!

Preface

Stand up now. Stand up and let the class know what you were just whispering
about to your friends. Stand up and let us all in on the joke.—An interaction
between a frustrated teacher and a disrespectful middle school student

We have often thought about interactions like this as symbolic—an exasper-
ated teacher and a rude youngster. It was the *stand up* part of the interaction
that was most memorable. Was the teacher trying to humiliate the student?
Was the teacher trying to illustrate how embarrassing it is to be whispered
about? Was the teacher trying to publicly chasten the student?

Most of all, we considered the *stand up* element of the degradation. We
thought about the young female student and how she would *withstand* the
demeaning reprimand as she did, in fact, reluctantly stand up. Or from another point of view, was the teacher merely *grandstanding*, in an effort to
reduce undesirable whispering?

The research on bullying often focuses on the perpetrator, the victim, and
the *bystander.* When teachers model classroom dynamics such as this are
they asking the rest of the class to be *bystanders* or *upstanders?* Yet, *standing up* can, at times, be positive as in the example of a debate and taking a
stance or a position.

Negative instances of classroom management abound, and yet strong,
positive examples are harder to showcase and more difficult to model. In
each of the documentary accounts in this book, teachers chose to *stand up*
and create *stand*ards for successful classroom management.

THE UNIVERSAL CHALLENGES OF CLASSROOM MANAGEMENT

Classroom management is often perceived as the most overwhelming challenge faced by new teachers; it may also continue to confront more experienced educators as they encounter a new group of youngsters or face a new set of demands. Mistakenly, classroom management is often associated with discipline. It is our belief—shared by the contributors of this volume—that classroom management is how *everything* is organized in an instructional environment for learning to take place:

* how instructional time is structured;
* how a designated place is established for resources, materials, and activities;
* how predictable and regular procedures are created and maintained;
* how daily routines and rituals are embraced; and ultimately
* how high student expectations are reinforced.

Successful classroom management is invariably tied to student engagement and empowerment: teachers who are singled out for excellent classroom management practices are often praised for successfully maintaining a strong instructional focus in their classes coupled with high levels of student engagement, empowerment, as well as management. Denti (2012) noted that student empowerment begins with "recognition and encouragement from proactive educators" (p. 8); as many of the chapters also demonstrate, consideration for students must be at the core of any classroom management strategy.

DOCUMENTARY ACCOUNTS AND EVIDENCE-BASED PRACTICES

In this volume, Carrie Rothstein-Fisch and Elise Trumbull discuss how culture-based assumptions may influence classroom interactions and invite readers to think outside the mold as they consider effective classroom management approaches for immigrant Latino students. In the next chapter, Marcia B. Imbeau and Carol Ann Tomlinson explain how to lead and manage a differentiated classroom, noting that change begins with a vision of what the teacher is trying to achieve.

Brittany L. Hott, Jennifer D. Walker, and Frederick J. Brigham offer insights into the implementation of self-management strategies and self-monitoring tools, so that secondary students may take a more active role in self-regulating their behavior and tracking their own progress. Next, Hillary Merk discusses the ideological shift in the literature from classroom discipline to classroom community building and what that means for diverse learners.

Additionally, Anneli Frelin invites us to visit a Swedish high school where the teacher leaves the traditional boundaries of the classroom and takes the students into the hallways to witness how to negotiate educational authority relationships outside of the typical classroom context. It is with the same encouraging tone that Lou Denti inspires us to offer choices, to provide extra support, and to share the message that every student is *worth the effort.*

The use of root metaphors for supporting student engagement is described by Terry Murray, focusing on academic and social-emotional learning for at-risk students. The *Board Game Project* he describes was developed as a means to help students reflect their personal stories. Ryan Flessner's chapter presents literature circles in the elementary language arts classroom as it documents how a significant shift in one teacher's philosophy of education led to a strong learning community. In this example, trust, respect, and student empowerment prevailed.

The design of a program for caring majority ambassadors is detailed by Karen Siris, as part of a plan for schools to truly embrace a caring culture. In a critical chapter, Jessica Minahan and Nancy Rappaport note that if students with anxiety are to succeed in school, they need a prescribed behavioral intervention plan that addresses anxiety, helps them learn alternative appropriate responses, and includes accommodations.

Next, Barbara Berté, Micheline Susan Malow, and Diane W. Gómez advocate the implementation of a warm demander pedagogy which supports the cultivation of teacher-student relationships built on respect and trust. This is followed by a chapter focusing on how to manage online classroom spaces by Jeffrey P. Drake and Jeanette L. Drake. Through their writing, we are reminded that online sources serve as the public square of the 21st century and that digital citizenship education is a priority for all educators.

Bettina L. Love shifts the focus to culturally relevant cyphers, and asks the reader to rethink classroom management through the lens of hip hop–based education. Similarly, Jon Nordmeyer and Peter Stelzer describe a *flipped* and *layered* classroom, which provides more time for individual, pair, and small group work within the class. Strong classroom management is described by Jennifer Lauria as she explains the power of caring, trust, and mutual respect.

Following is a chapter in which strategies to increase student collaboration—while implementing the Common Core State Standards—are proposed by Maria G. Dove and Vicky Giouroukakis. Enhancing the vision of positive management is accomplished by Luanna H. Meyer and Ian M. Evans, who describe the role of restorative classroom discipline as a means to diffuse conflict in the classroom.

Martha Edelson and Lori Langer de Ramirez outline ways to establish and to maintain a positive classroom culture in the middle school and provide parameters for a successful learning environment. Howard M. Knoff takes an organizational perspective and explains what positive behavioral supports are needed at the system, school, and staff levels. Last but not least, Marie Menna Pagliaro takes the reader step by step through the challenges of providing a 21st century classroom, and examines new perspectives needed for learning environments that yield innovation and success. Bryan Harris, in the Afterword, presents key ideas from research and practice on how to build resiliency for students and teachers in the future.

Classroom management continues to be one of the most difficult aspects of teaching for both new and more experienced educators alike. Our hope is that sharing stories of successful practices—as documented in this final volume—will prove to be an authentic way to support others in the profession.

COMPLETING THE *BREAKING THE MOLD* SERIES

This is the fifth and final book of the *Breaking the Mold* series. Through this project, we have highlighted *innovative* practices that have been created, modeled, adapted, and publicized by teachers throughout the world. In total, there have been over 250 authors in over 130 chapters, and they were all focused on sharing their success stories as a means of improving education.

We often joke that we have not yet completely "Broken the Mold" and there are still so many stories that can inspire and motivate teachers and students to be the best that they can be. However, our work on the series has come to an end, although our quest to improve the quality of education for *all* students will be ongoing. Thank you for being part of this journey.

REFERENCES

Denti, L. (2012). *Proactive classroom management K-8: A practical guide to empower students and teachers*. Thousand Oaks, CA: Corwin Press.

Chapter One

Thinking Outside the Mold: How Teachers Learned to Make Classroom Management Work for Their Immigrant Latino Students

Carrie Rothstein-Fisch and Elise Trumbull

In a second-grade classroom, Mrs. Blaine (a pseudonym) is conducting a lesson and asking her students to respond to questions. The children begin to whisper answers to each other. The teacher's response is "I have heard people whispering and I really don't like it because why? They need to learn by themselves and you really aren't helping them learn" (Isaac, 1999, p. 34). In another classroom, Mrs. Pérez (a teacher from the Bridging Cultures project, discussed below) is conducting a language arts lesson with her third-grade children sitting on the rug.

Noticing that one student seems to be answering most of the questions, she suggests, "Why don't you whisper the answer to a friend?" (Rothstein-Fisch & Trumbull, 2008, p. 147). These two teachers demonstrate contrasting views of how students learn and how they should behave in the classroom.

Mrs. Blaine's belief about how children learn reflects the mainstream view: Learning is largely an individual matter, and knowledge is possessed by the individual. Mrs. Pérez's belief about how children learn is reflective of her students' Mexican American culture, where learning is a group process and knowledge is possessed by or distributed among the group. These two different views led one teacher to chastise children for a behavior that another teacher encouraged.

Increasingly, classrooms in the United States are places where different cultures meet and interact. There is the culture of the school and the culture of the teacher, both most often reflecting European American *mainstream*

1

values (Gay, 2006; Hollins, 1996). We consider this the typical mold for most teaching; however, children from other cultures may have a mold for learning that has a completely different shape.

WHAT IS CULTURE?

When we speak of culture, we refer to the systems of values, beliefs, and ways of knowing that guide communities of people in their daily lives. As educational researchers, we focus in particular on how these people approach learning and problem-solving, how they construct knowledge, and how they pass ideas and practices to future generations (Rothstein-Fisch & Trumbull, 2008).

Cultures are associated with different notions of how students learn best; how they should behave; how to meet the expectations of the school; and what roles teachers, students, and parents should play. However, these aspects of culture are generally invisible.

Educators may believe that there is one right way to organize and manage a classroom without recognizing that their strategies are a cultural enterprise. In this chapter—through examples from actual elementary school classrooms—we explore how to make classroom organization and management work better for diverse groups of students by tapping their cultural strengths.

Our premise is that teachers need to become more aware not only of their students' cultures but also of their own, because their culture-based assumptions influence every classroom decision they make. Learning about others' cultures can appear to be a daunting task. For example, one teacher recalled:

> I wanted to understand my students better, so I started studying Mexican culture. Then I realized that the children in my class came from so many distinct regions of Mexico, Central and South America, each with differing histories and traditions. I knew that I would never know enough. I had to give up trying. (Rothstein-Fisch & Trumbull, 2008, p. 8)

The lament of this teacher is often echoed by educators who believe that culture is too vast and complex a topic to be understood. Learning about one's own culture can seem equally challenging; many mainstream educators do not, in fact, see themselves as "having a culture."

But what if there were a relatively simple framework for understanding some of the most important differences between cultures? Would teachers be able to use such a framework to understand the cultural perspectives of their students and themselves and, in the process, make their classrooms more effective learning environments for their students?

THE INDIVIDUALISM-COLLECTIVISM FRAMEWORK

The individualism-collectivism framework captures fundamental differences between U.S. mainstream culture and the cultures of many immigrant and minority students (Greenfield, 1994). The mainstream culture of the United States, with its primarily Western European origins, is individualistic: The values of independence, individual responsibility and achievement, self-expression, promotion of self-esteem, and individual ownership of property are reflected in families' child-rearing practices.

In contrast, many other cultures, with roots in Asia, Central and South America, and Africa are collectivistic: The values of interdependence, group responsibility and achievement, respect for elders, personal modesty, and shared property are reflected in families' child-rearing practices.

The distinction between these two cultural value systems lies not in absolutes but in the degree of emphasis accorded to each. No culture or family is exclusively individualistic or collectivistic; however, in any group, patterns of behavior based on shared values and beliefs are observable. In cultures that emphasize the group over the individual, one is likely to see parents helping their children and encouraging their children to help each other, to share possessions, to work hard for the benefit of the family or social group, and to be modest about personal achievements.

In cultures that emphasize the individual over the group, one is likely to observe parents encouraging their children to do things for themselves, to take care of their personal property, to work hard to achieve, and to take pride in their accomplishments. The implicit cultural mold for schools is strongly individualistic. Students are expected to work independently, compete with each other, maintain their own personal property, and complete learning tasks by themselves. Even when teachers do use a cooperative learning strategy, they typically arrange for students to take individual roles and to be graded individually.

Classroom management is built on these foundational beliefs. This is highlighted in the example above where Mrs. Blaine responds to children's attempts to help each other by admonishing them. It is likely that she does not see how whispering might confer advantage on both students, or she may perceive that talking is automatically an indicator of students' being off task.

In contrast, Mrs. Pérez understood that displaying modesty by not speaking out and helping a fellow student are cultural norms for her immigrant Latino students. Skillfully, she leveraged her knowledge of the children's desire to help others to encourage a child who might otherwise be reluctant to display her developing oral language skills. Mrs. Blaine may be thwarting children's learning, while Mrs. Pérez is likely promoting their learning, guided by her knowledge of the children's culture.

THE BRIDGING CULTURES™ PROJECT

Based on research targeting immigrant Latino students, their parents, and their teachers (Greenfield, Quiroz, & Raeff, 2000; Raeff, Greenfield, & Quiroz, 2000), we launched the Bridging Cultures Project with our fellow researchers Patricia Marks Greenfield and Blanca Quiroz. We wondered, "What would teachers do if they were offered the framework of individualism-collectivism for understanding cultures?" We recruited seven elementary school teachers from five schools in the greater Los Angeles area who were teaching in bilingual Spanish-English classrooms.

An important part of our selection process was identifying teachers with a preexisting interest in meeting the needs of large numbers of Latino students. The teachers were all very experienced (with an average of 12.7 years of teaching); four of the seven identified themselves as Latino, while the other three identified themselves as European American. By chance, the teachers represented the full range of grade levels in K–5. Three workshops were held over a period of four months.

In the first workshop, teachers were asked to solve home- and school-based cultural dilemmas represented in short written scenarios (Raeff et al., 2000). Much to their own surprise, they responded in strongly individualistic ways. Even the Latino teachers tended to solve the dilemmas from an individualistic perspective.

The new awareness of her mainstream cultural stance caused one Latino teacher to rethink her own educational values:

> As an immigrant from Mexico myself, I can see how I have had to fight my own collectivistic upbringing to be successful in U.S. schools. . . . Now we need to tap our own cultural knowledge for the sake of our students.

Without an explicit framework for understanding the differences between individualism and collectivism, these teachers were resolving conflicts in a strongly individualistic way. Another teacher commented, "For me, it's just being aware of the differences, of what we are doing. It gives a name to what we're doing. I don't think I would have known how to talk about this before" (Trumbull, Diaz-Meza, Hasan, & Rothstein-Fisch, 2000, pp. 10–11).

Between the first and second workshops, teachers were asked to observe in their schools for evidence of both individualistic and collectivistic practices. In the second workshop, they were abuzz with examples of largely individualistic practices reflecting classroom rules. Their assignment between workshops two and three was to make a change in their classroom of their own design and based on their own concerns. The teachers reported on these changes in detail at the third meeting.

At the end of the professional development workshops, teachers were asked to respond to four more scenarios used in the original research (Raeff et al., 2000). Sure enough, the teachers dramatically shifted their thinking from a strongly individualistic one (86%) to one that balanced individualism (21%) with collectivism (57%) or a combination of both perspectives (21%).

As a result of three half-day workshops, teachers broke the mold of organizing their classes from a single perspective (individualism) and began to seek new ways to orchestrate classroom management. The group of teachers and core researchers continued to meet every few months over a period of five years (Trumbull et al., 2000) to discuss how the teachers continued to create new ways to organize teaching and learning.

It is important to note that all the examples cited in this chapter come from the teachers' own inventions. Nothing was ever suggested or prescribed by the core researchers. Examples come from three sources: (a) teachers' contributions at workshops and research meetings, (b) direct observations by researchers during classrooms visits, and (c) in-depth interviews, often lasting as long as two hours, with teachers. Let us return to the examples of whispering. Mrs. Blaine is a non–Bridging Cultures teacher, whereas Mrs. Pérez is a Bridging Cultures teacher.

Mrs. Blaine divided her class into two groups for math. A representative from each team came up to work on the same addition problem, often prompting the students to shout out, "oooh," indicating the kinds of pressure this evoked. Some even positioned themselves as if they were praying. The two students at the board competed with each other without any assistance from their team. According to Isaac (1999), there were great signs of stress among the children, both those at the board and those who may have feared they were next. Though on the surface this may have seemed like a group activity, it was actually highly individualized and competitive.

Mrs. Pérez also assigned children to groups in her math lesson. However in her class, children were organized by tables, and the goal was to collect 1,000 of one particular item selected by the group at that table. Children would then be asked to organize the items in various ways. Mrs. Pérez asked each group what item they had decided to collect, and children offered to help other groups, saying things like, "I can bring in pennies to help table 3" or "I can bring in rocks." Other tables decided to collect nails, marbles, and crayons.

During the lesson, students worked together to decide the best way to group their objects for easy inventory. One group started by making groups of 100 objects but realized that counting to 100 was difficult, so they discussed their options and decided to group by 25. Other groups counted by factors of 10, 20, 50, and 100. In the second part of the lesson, the children reported on how many objects they had, how they had grouped them, and how many more they needed. The students learned the various ways to count by factors to the number 1,000.

They also were encouraged to help others by providing the objects needed for all the groups to reach the goal. In this example, the children worked both in small groups and as a whole, helping their classmates. Within a short period of time, every group had successfully gathered 1,000 objects and could articulate how the items were gathered, who helped, how they sorted and counted, and why one method of factoring may have worked better than others they tried.

In Mrs. Pérez's class, all the children succeeded by helping each other: There were no losers, no competition to see who could be the first to get all 1,000 items, and no overt reward other than the joy of learning and sharing new ideas with others. In contrast to Mrs. Blaine, Mrs. Pérez did not have students who felt like failures because they had botched the task.

MANAGEMENT AND ORGANIZATION: MOLDING CLASSROOM PRACTICES TO STUDENT NEEDS

Over the five years of the Project, teachers' innovations often focused on changes affecting classroom organization and management. Not only did they make changes in classroom rules and rewards (Rothstein-Fisch & Trumbull, 2008), they also found themselves relating differently to parents and taking a different approach to students helping and sharing in the classroom. A few examples about monitors and classroom rules will demonstrate how teachers broke the mold of their previous practices learned primarily through their teacher training courses.

Classroom Monitors

One of the first changes that many teachers made was in their organization of classroom monitors, where the maxim "one person-one job" was causing problems for many of the teachers because children wanted to help their friends. Instead of spending class time reminding children NOT to help each other, the teachers changed the rules. One teacher, Mr. Mercado, said, "I had individual monitors, and now [I have] group monitors, and that works more smoothly than what I had before. I am more conscious about why certain things work" (Rothstein-Fisch & Trumbull, 2008, p. 85).

Similarly, Mrs. Pérez reconsidered the individualistic mold of thinking about helpers: "I used to be very resistant to having more than one child out of the classroom at once. It would bother me when they asked for a friend to go with them to do an errand," she said (Rothstein-Fisch & Trumbull, 2008, p. 86). After her involvement with the Bridging Cultures Project, she reported that students' preferences to take a friend with them was not coming from a desire to be off task, but might more likely be the cultural value of helping, "Yeah, of course, it is much better to have someone with you. I never thought of that [before] and I was just resistant to it" (p. 86).

Classroom Rules

In Ms. Altchech's fourth-grade class, rules were posted on the wall, including; "I will raise my hand for permission to speak or leave my seat" and "I will keep my hands, feet, and objects to myself." Perhaps realizing that her largely Latino students often wanted to help their friends, she eliminated the rule for permission to speak as well as the overt rule against sharing. Instead, the new rules were reduced to only two requirements: "Be respectful" and "Be serious about learning."

Reflected in all the teachers' changes in rules was the notion of respect. When respect becomes a central point of classroom organization, it allows children to wait their turn, honor the role of the other learners, and treat the teacher with deference. Respect is understood in the context of the home environment, as both broader and deeper than it is in the dominant culture (Valdés, 1996).

FINAL COMMENTS

While the original focus of the Bridging Cultures Project was not classroom management, it became a topic of interest, as we reviewed the data we had collected. We were struck by the fact that in over 40 hours of observation there were only nine instances of discipline (defined as "a reprimand or threat"), and eight of those were observed in a single classroom on the day before the students were going on vacation.

Although we do not have documentation of the teachers' classroom management before their introduction to the framework of individualism and collectivism, we hypothesize that their documented changes in thinking about culture were indeed associated with changes in their management practices. In any case, their management practices were clearly culturally responsive and can be understood with reference to the individualism-collectivism framework.

The examples we use here are from classrooms of mostly Latino students—those whose families came from Mexico or Central America. But students with African, Asian, and American Indian roots have much in common with these Latino students: Their cultures are in general far more collectivistic than the mainstream culture of the United States (Greenfield, 1994). But understanding of specific cultural contexts depends upon more direction experience and interaction. Visiting students' communities, participating in community events, and working with parent volunteers will help teachers build that kind of understanding.

The individualism-collectivism framework can be a starting point for teachers' observations—of both themselves and their students. It can help teachers formulate questions for family members about their goals and expectations for their children. In our experience, increased cultural awareness is almost immediately useful to teachers in designing successful classroom management strategies and learning activities.

Authors' Note

The Bridging Cultures Project™ is a registered trademark of WestEd, licensed to the four core researchers: Patricia M. Greenfield (UCLA), Blanca Quiroz (SEDL, Austin, TX), Carrie Rothstein-Fisch (California State University, Northbridge) and Elise Trumball (Educational Consultant, Oakland, California). The seven elementary teachers who have been part of the Bridging Cultures Project are Marie Altchech, Catherine Daley, Kathryn Eyler, Elvia Hernandez, Giancarlo Mercado, Amada Perez, and Pearl Saitzyk. The original research was funded by the Office of Educational Research and Improvement of the U.S. Department of Education through WestEd, with additional funding from California State University, Northridge, the A. L. Mailman Family Foundation, and the Sage Foundation.

REFERENCES

Gay, G. (2006). Connections between classroom management and culturally responsive teaching. In C. M. Evertson & C. S. Weinstein (Eds.), *Handbook of classroom management: Research, practice, and contemporary issues* (pp. 343–370). Mahwah, NJ: Lawrence Erlbaum.

Greenfield, P. M. (1994). Independence and interdependence as developmental scripts: Implications for theory, research, and practice. In P. M. Greenfield & R. R. Cocking (Eds.), *Cross-cultural roots of minority child development* (pp. 1–37). Mahwah, NJ: Lawrence Erlbaum.

Greenfield, P. M., Quiroz, B., & Raeff, C. (2000). Cross-cultural conflict and harmony in the social construction of the child. In S. Harkness, C. Raeff, & C. M. Super (Eds.), Variability in the social construction of the child. *New Directions for Child and Adolescent Development, 87,* 93–108.

Hollins, E. (1996). *Culture in school learning: Revealing the deep meaning.* Mahwah, NJ: Lawrence Erlbaum.

Isaac, A. R. (1999). How teachers' cultural ideologies influence children's relations inside the classroom: The effects of a cultural awareness teacher training program in two classrooms. Psychology Honors Thesis. Unpublished manuscript. University of California, Los Angeles.

Raeff, C., Greenfield, P. M., & Quiroz, B. (2000). Conceptualizing interpersonal relationships in the cultural contexts of individualism and collectivism. In S. Harkness, C. Raeff, & C. M. Super (Eds.), Variability in the social construction of the child. *New Directions for Child and Adolescent Development, 87,* 59–74.

Rothstein-Fisch, C., & Trumbull, E. (2008). *Managing diverse classrooms: How to build on students' cultural strengths.* Alexandria, VA: Association for Supervision and Curriculum Development.

Trumbull, E., Diaz-Meza, R., Hasan, A., & Rothstein-Fisch, C. (2000). *The Bridging Cultures Project: Five-year report* 1996–2000. San Francisco, CA: WestEd.

Valdés, G. (1996). *Con respeto: Bridging the distances between culturally diverse families and schools, an ethnographic portrait.* New York, NY: Teachers College Press.

Chapter Two

Managing a Differentiated Classroom

Marcia B. Imbeau and Carol Ann Tomlinson

Mr. Williams is about to begin his career as a teacher. In his mind, he frequently plays and replays several scenarios related to classroom management. This aspect of his new role is the most worrisome to him. He has read the work of numerous experts on classroom management who often disagree considerably on what effective classroom management looks like and how a teacher achieves it.

In one scenario, he is careful to lay out rules for his students on the first day of school and is faithful in ensuring that all students follow those rules without exception. He is also consistent in responding to infractions with pre-established consequences, noting with small hash marks on a behavior management chart whoever breaks a rule.

He makes sure students are seated by the time of a designated signal. He ensures that students begin their task together when he finishes the explanation of that work and he emphasizes the importance of everyone completing work on time. He has arranged the furniture, student seating, and materials in the room to minimize student movement. If he can get those elements right, he muses, he will be okay with classroom management—or he hopes so.

In the second scenario, he sees his students working with focus on tasks he has assigned. Some of the students are working alone and some are working with peers. That gives him time to meet with small groups of students or to move among students to see how they are progressing and to coach them as he does. Students occasionally come to him to ask a question or ask a peer. Occasionally a student also moves around to get or return materials. There is conversation in the room, but it seems purposeful.

Somehow, the second classroom is the one in which he would like to be a student. It feels more comfortable to him as a teacher, also. He is not quite sure where the image of the second classroom comes from, however. He has had more personal experience with the first one. And maybe the first scenario is the only realistic one. In any case, as a new teacher, he is not sure how he would design and implement the more student-friendly classroom.

CLASSROOM MANAGEMENT AND THE PHILOSOPHY OF DIFFERENTIATION

Differentiated instruction is as much a philosophy of teaching as it is a model for teaching. It is rooted in the premise that student variance is both normal and desirable and that teachers who are respectful of students' learning needs proactively plan for and attend to those needs with the goal of offering all students maximum opportunity to develop their potential as learners.

The model requires teacher attention to five key classroom elements in ways that reflect current best thinking on the art and science of teaching (National Research Council, 2000; Hattie, 2009, 2012) so that practice with each element reinforces the intent of the other elements.

The five classroom elements are the following:

1. a learning environment that emphasizes a growth mindset for teacher and students, teacher-student connections, and a sense of team or community among members;
2. curriculum with clearly articulated learning goals, designed to engage learners, focused on student understanding, and *teaching up*;
3. formative assessment used to guide the teacher's instructional planning and students' ownership of learning;
4. teacher responsiveness to student variance in readiness, interest, and learning profile or learning preferences; and
5. classroom management designed to create an orderly, flexible environment that enables teachers to implement more than one approach to teaching and learning when that would likely facilitate student development (Sousa & Tomlinson, 2011; Tomlinson & Imbeau, 2010, 2012; Tomlinson & McTighe, 2006; Tomlinson & Moon, 2013).

Guidelines for managing a differentiated classroom are integral to and reflective of the student-focused nature of the model. Effective management in a differentiated classroom contributes to a learning environment in which students are challenged, supported in meeting that challenge, and empowered as learners. It provides the context for student engagement with complex ideas and skills, for making sense of those ideas and skills, and for using the ideas and skills in meaningful contexts.

Deciding how to manage a differentiated classroom allows for teachers to systematically address the needs of a broad variety of learners and creates opportunity for students to be full partners in their own learning success as well as that of their peers. It is useful to consider the nature of classroom management for differentiation in three categories:

1. the teacher as leader,
2. students as the teacher's partners in making the classroom work, and
3. the process of establishing and refining an orderly, flexible classroom.

LEAD FIRST

It is likely that many teachers think of classroom management as a synonym for *control*. From that perspective, managing the classroom focuses primary attention on managing students—making sure the students are generally quiet and still, and that they start and stop assignments at the same time.

The concept of *controlling* or *managing* learners is flawed on several levels. First, like most humans, young people often do not like to feel *managed* or *controlled*. Equating classroom management with *crowd control* communicates a lack of trust in students and establishes an almost adversarial relationship between teacher and learner. Further, it suggests that primary value is placed on order and predictability rather than on students' learning needs.

Differentiation advises that teachers should first *lead students*, and then *manage the procedures and processes* that enable students to work both collaboratively and more independently.

The traits of strong leaders are relatively stable across contexts. Among the most important of those traits are:

- having a vision about which the leader is passionate,
- effectively communicating the vision to others,
- inspiring others to be part of the vision,
- accepting responsibility for the success of followers,
- respecting and working collaboratively with followers,
- empowering followers, and
- pursuing the vision courageously and persistently.

Such leaders work from key principles and aspire to live out those principles. They are reflective and learn from experiences of their own as well as those they share with followers. These attributes are evident in teachers who seek to lead students to be their partners in *responsive* teaching and learning.

Leading students in a differentiated classroom means sharing with them in words and actions the teacher's belief that every person in the classroom is unique and valuable and that helping each person become the best he or she can be is a worthy goal. The teacher's words and actions throughout the year communicate that:

1. classrooms should be designed to work for all of the students in them,
2. the teacher works hard each day toward that goal,
3. achieving the goal is far more likely if the teacher and students work together to make sure that everyone has the support necessary to succeed with challenging work, and
4. the teacher genuinely wants to work with the class to create routines and procedures that help each student do his or her best work and to grow as fully as possible.

This message both stems from and contributes to a relationship of trust and interdependence in the classroom between teacher and student and between student and student. It conveys the conviction that this place is *our* classroom and we have the capacity to make it a powerful place for each and every individual in the classroom.

The compelling message helps everyone reflect on the reality that students inevitably enter learning experiences at different points and that where they enter is never as important as how hard they work to move ahead. The teacher's goal—they should come to understand—is to work every day to help each learner take his or her next step toward important goals. The teacher takes that goal quite seriously and calls on students to do the same.

The teacher who *leads* in a differentiated classroom makes clear to students that he or she is trustworthy because the students' best interests are at the core of everything that happens in the classroom. As van Manen (1991) expressed the idea,

> Leading means going first, and in going first, you can trust me, for I have tested the ice. I have lived. I now know something of the rewards as well as the trappings of growing toward adulthood and making a world for yourself. Although the going first is no guarantee of success (because the world is not without risks and dangers), in the pedagogical relationship, there is a more fundamental guarantee: No matter what, I am here. And you can count on me. (p. 38)

Leaders in differentiated classrooms can begin to engage students in considering the vision of a classroom designed to support the success of each student through conversations. This might involve having students share their positive and negative experiences as learners and the teacher doing the same both as a learner and a teacher.

Other conversations might include sharing survey data that make clear the variety of students' likes and dislikes, strengths and weaknesses, and approaches to learning in the classroom; using excerpts from children's literature or biographies; role plays, and a variety of other approaches. The conversation should continue throughout the year—generally briefly, but often enough so that students can both understand and contribute to the teacher's vision for them.

EMPOWER STUDENTS

Certainly a primary goal of any classroom ought to be ensuring that students develop competencies with critical content. In fact, the aim of differentiation is to create a context in which that is possible for a broad range of students in a single classroom. Yet, students are not simply repositories of information and practicers of skills. They need also to develop as responsible stewards of their own learning, to think critically, to grow in respect for the world around them, to value increasingly perspectives other than their own, to communicate effectively, and so on.

Ways in which teachers conceive and design curriculum and instruction either contribute to or inhibit growth in those areas. Likewise, ways in which teachers conceive of and execute classroom leadership and management also support or curb student development. As the teacher in a differentiated classroom leads, he or she communicates to students important messages such as the following:

- You are unique and valuable and, therefore, have worthwhile things to contribute to our class. We're counting on you to make those contributions.
- You have experiences that help you connect with what we are studying and that can help others connect as well.
- When you work hard and wisely in this place, you will see yourself grow.
- You also play a key role in helping peers work hard and wisely so they can grow as well.
- All of us will celebrate growth in any of us and in the group as a whole.
- You have the capacity and the responsibility to contribute to the architecture of a classroom that respects both our differences and our similarities.
- I will do my best as a teacher to help you grow as much as you can in this place. I am counting on you to help me do my best and to help your classmates do their best as well.

Toward that goal of helping students develop increasing autonomy as learners who are invested in their own success and that of peers, the teacher ensures that students:

- are known, respected, and heard;

- are consistently aware of essential learning goals and standards of quality work;
- understand and contribute to the teacher's innovative vision for the classroom;
- develop habits of mind and work that reflect those of successful people including communicating with purpose, listening to understand, questioning, gathering information, striving for accuracy, seeking and using feedback to learn, thinking about thinking, persistence in the face of difficulty, and valuing learning (Costa & Kallick, 2000);
- use formative assessment information to understand their current points of development relative to essential learning goals and standards of quality as well as to plan for their continuing development in the short term and longer term;
- learn how to use and provide feedback that supports peer success;
- learn how to collaborate effectively with peers and how to intercede when work with peers is not proceeding in a productive manner;
- contribute to classroom routines that facilitate differentiation and student success; and
- have opportunity to provide frequent input on ways in which teaching, learning, and the flow of the classroom are serving them well or inhibiting their development as learners and as people.

In effectively differentiated classrooms, all of the classroom elements—environment, curriculum, assessment, instruction, and classroom management—are constructed to empower and guide students to assume increasing responsibility for their academic success and for their decisions and actions as human beings in general. Therefore, students in such classrooms are not passive recipients of an education that *happens to them*, but rather key players in the great majority of transactions that happen in class.

As Csikszentmihalyi (2008) observed, young people who grow up in situations that facilitate clarity of goals, feelings of control, concentration on the task at hand, intrinsic motivation, and challenge have a better chance to order their lives in ways that make learning satisfying and motivating.

MANAGE DETAILS

Whereas the role of a leader in a classroom is to inspire and support students (people) to contribute to a vision, the role of teacher as manager has a different emphasis. In that role, the teacher must provide structure, stability, and predictability that aims not for standardization and uniformity but at flexibility in ways students can achieve critical outcomes. In other words, the teacher moves between the role of leading people and managing routines and processes.

Differentiated classrooms should never be disorderly, unpredictable, or chaotic. Rather, they should be both dependable and open. Calkins (1983) offered support for this idea stating:

> It is significant to realize that the most creative environments in our society are not the ever-changing ones. The artist's studio, the researcher's laboratory, the scholar's library are each kept deliberately simple so as to support the complexities of the work in progress. They are deliberately kept predictable so the unpredictable can happen. (p. 32)

To that end, teachers, with the assistance of students, need to ensure that guidelines are in place for things such as: managing general classroom behavior, moving around the classroom to get and return materials, obtaining help when the teacher is working with individuals or small groups, providing help to peers in appropriate ways and at appropriate times, monitoring noise when collaborating with others, working in places like computer stations or centers, starting and stopping class efficiently and effectively, and focusing on one's own work rather than on the work of others.

A FEW TIPS

There are several areas of the classroom operation that effective teachers routinely consider in order to make sure it works for everyone. For those who are new to this way of teaching and learning, a few practical suggestions to get started are as follows:

1. Describe procedures and processes clearly to students as well as help them to understand the rationale for the procedures.
2. Choose a pace of implementation that is slow enough for both students and teacher to feel comfortable and confident.
3. Review regularly with students how a routine or process was supposed to work and debrief on the degree to which it worked as it should.
4. Experiment with new routines and procedures with confidence in your capability to refine your ideas based on student feedback.
5. Reflect often on the degree to which your practice of implementing routines and procedures aligns with the vision you initially had for your classroom and make adjustments when needed.

A REASONED CHOICE

Determining how to lead and manage a differentiated classroom begins with a vision of what the teacher is trying to achieve. Mr. Williams decided that if he believed all learners should be able to work to their maximum potential, he needed to guide students and organize the classroom in a way that enabled him to address the students' diverse learning needs. He understood that his actions in classroom management would signal students that he believed in—and was willing to invest in—their capacity to contribute to their own success and that of their peers.

This approach to leadership and management, he concluded, would make the classroom both more student-focused and more learning-focused. He came to believe over time that teachers who actively seek ways to improve the school experience for each of their students find greater satisfaction and joy in their work—as do the students they lead.

REFERENCES

Calkins, L. (1983). *Lessons from a child: On the teaching and learning of writing*. Portsmouth, NH: Heinemann.

Costa, A., & Kallick, B. (2000). *Discovering and exploring habits of mind*. Alexandria, VA: ASCD.

Csikszentmihalyi, M. (2008). *Flow: The psychology of optimal experience*. New York, NY: Harper Perennial Modern Classics.

Hattie, J. (2009). *Visible learning: A synthesis of over 800 meta-analyses relating to achievement*. New York, NY: Routledge.

Hattie, J. (2012). *Visible learning for teachers: Maximizing impact on learning*. New York, NY: Routledge.

National Research Council. (2000). *How people learn: Brain, mind, experience, and school*. Washington, DC: National Academy Press.

Sousa, D. A., & Tomlinson, C. A. (2011). *Differentiation and the brain: How neuroscience supports the learner-friendly classroom*. Bloomington, IN: Solution Tree Press.

Tomlinson, C. A., & Imbeau, M. B. (2010). *Leading and managing a differentiated classroom*. Alexandria, VA: ASCD.

Tomlinson, C. A., & Imbeau, M. B. (2012). Differentiated instruction: An integration of theory and practice. In B. Irby, G. Brown, R. Lara-Alecio, & S. Jackson (Eds.), *Handbook of educational theories* (pp. 1081–1101). Charlotte, NC: Information Age Publishing.

Tomlinson, C. A., & McTighe, J. (2006). *Integrating differentiated instruction and understanding by design: Connecting content and kids*. Alexandria, VA: ASCD.

Tomlinson, C. A., & Moon, T. (2013). *Assessment in a differentiated classroom: A guide for student success*. Alexandria, VA: ASCD.

van Manen, M. (1991). *The tact of teaching: Toward a pedagogy of thoughtfulness*. Albany, NY: State University of New York.

Chapter Three

Implementing Self-Management Strategies in the Secondary Classroom

Brittany L. Hott, Jennifer D. Walker, and Frederick J. Brigham

MEET LILLIAN

On any given day at Campbell Middle School, Lillian could be found in the front office, discipline referral in hand. Despite the school and staff commitment to a streamlined Response to Intervention (RTI) tiered approach for both academics and behavior, Lillian continued to challenge her teachers and the administration with problematic behavior.

Traditional approaches, including differentiated instruction, positive reinforcement, clear and consistent expectations, as well as pre-established procedures and consequences, were largely ineffective with Lillian. Combined with impulsive and disruptive behavior, Lillian struggled with mathematics, particularly when presented with independent tasks.

The staff at Campbell Middle School were desperate for an intervention that would increase Lillian's academic engagement. The teachers were searching for something that could be used across settings and would increase her motivation to work independently.

POSITIVE BEHAVIOR SUPPORT SYSTEMS

When positive behavioral support systems are implemented with fidelity, there is often a need to focus on individual students who require additional supports for school success (Brigham & Brigham, 2010; Kauffman & Brigham, 2009). Through the systematic use of behavioral assessment and strategy development, students can achieve success in managing their behaviors and developing essential skills for transition into adulthood. *Self-monitoring* is a powerful, research-based strategy that shifts the responsibility of behavioral regulation from staff to the student (Hott & Walker, 2012; Sheffield & Waller, 2010).

Teachers at the secondary level are charged with ensuring that their students master content while simultaneously supporting individual academic and behavioral needs. While traditional pedagogy has relied on teacher-initiated tools to manage classroom behavior, a rich body of research demonstrates that shifting from teacher-driven strategies to student-initiated strategies, such as self-monitoring, can facilitate academic and social development (Agran, King-Sears, Wehmeyer, & Copeland, 2003; Ganz, 2008; Hott & Walker, 2012).

Therefore, teachers should consider using self-monitoring techniques to assist students with the development of internal regulation and, thereby, their independence and self-determination.

BEHAVIORAL TERMS

Prior to implementing a self-monitoring system, it is important to develop an understanding of common behavioral terms. Self-regulation is a critical component of child development that reconciles external influences and provides a foundation for behavioral actions. More specifically, self-regulation refers to the degree to which students actively and responsibly participate in their own learning (Zimmerman, 2008).

Two elements, self-management and self-monitoring are critical components necessary for self-regulation. Self-management is the process by which individuals manage their behavior and self-monitoring is a tool that a student can use to track academic or behavioral progress.

Although most students learn self-regulation without special instruction, others need interventions and supports to develop the key skills.

More specifically, self-monitoring can assist students with developing personal initiative, perseverance, and adaptive skills (Zimmerman, 2008). However, in order for students to successfully self-regulate, a number of fundamental phases must occur. These phases include the *forethought phase, performance phase,* and *self-reflection phase* (Kitsantas & Zimmerman, 2009). Self-regulated learners are able to proactively incorporate self-regulation processes, task strategies, and self-motivational beliefs. These phases are cyclical in nature and utilize internal feedback from previous learning experiences to make adjustments in future learning attempts.

Self-monitoring can assist students with and without disabilities (Ganz, 2008) in a variety of settings (Sheffield & Waller, 2010). Specifically, self-monitoring can lead to increases in compliance, organization skills, and academic task engagement. When implemented with fidelity, self-monitoring has the potential to influence both student achievement and social development.

SPECIALIZED SUPPORTS

Like Lillian, some students require individualized supports to function in the school environment. It is critical that supports fit within the school management system and meet the needs of the individual student. The first step is to determine if a student can independently complete the skill at some point (King-Sears, 2008). While Lillian's behavior was quite disruptive and often led to removal from the classroom, she had demonstrated the ability to complete some assignments independently and request help as needed.

However, if the tasks to be completed through self-regulation are not yet within the student's grasp, self-monitoring training is premature, at least for the task under consideration. In such cases, additional instruction in the to-be-learned skill or material, rather than behavioral intervention, is required. When the student has sufficient mastery of the to-be-learned target to regulate his or her performance, self-monitoring training can be valuable.

The self-monitoring process involves a student learning to assess and record whether a particular behavior has occurred. Both self-monitoring of attention (SMA) and self-monitoring of performance (SMP) can improve self-regulation. While there are varying definitions, SMA typically involves a student monitoring behaviors such as on-task, task engagement, or aggression. Consequently, SMP involves a student monitoring his or her academic progress. For example, SMP is often described in terms of number of words a student has written or the number of math problems a student has completed.

In Lillian's case, the team moved swiftly to individualize support for her behavioral challenges and completed a functional behavioral assessment (FBA). In a functional behavioral assessment, a team of professionals, which may include general or special education teachers, school administrators, parents, related service personnel, and students, convene to determine target behaviors of concern and identify possible triggers of the behavior, as well as conditions that support undesirable behavior or interfere with desirable behavior (Ingram, Lewis-Palmer, & Sugai, 2005).

A systematic collection and review of data—including reviewing the student file, collecting data on the behavior of concern, interviewing pertinent team members, and behavioral charting—occurs. Following sufficient data collection, the team determines the possible function of the behavior and identifies a more desirable replacement behavior that can be explicitly taught to the student.

FBA procedures assume that people exhibit behaviors to either obtain something they desire or to escape something undesirable. While many students exhibit attention or performance deficits, some students, like Lillian, exhibit both. In Lillian's case, it was determined that she accurately completed English and reading tasks within the time frame established by the instructor but that she struggled with mathematics. To address these issues, Lillian's team implemented ten steps focused on developing a self-monitoring system that could easily be executed in her general education classrooms.

1. *Determine target behaviors.* Mr. Peter, Lillian's classroom teacher, used a chart to determine specific behaviors of concern for Lillian. To most effectively target the behaviors, Mr. Peter carefully outlined the behaviors in a measurable, observable, and objective format.

   For an outside observer, the behaviors were defined in such a way that they were easily understood based on a concise and descriptive definition. In addition to charting behaviors and clearly outlining their definitions, Mr. Peter solicited Lillian's input, thereby engaging her in the process and enhancing her ownership and interest.

2. *Determine the frequency, duration, latency, and intensity of behavior.* This determination prompted Mr. Peter's selection of a data collection system. Through event recording, interval/time sampling, latency recording, and/or duration recording, Mr. Peter was able to establish a baseline, which provided a starting point for goal setting. The frequency, duration, latency, and intensity of the behavior of concern were all encompassed in the baseline information.

   Much like the definition of the behavior of concern, the data were as specific as possible, presenting a clear and concise picture of the behavior of concern. Once a behavior was identified along with a measurement system, Mr. Peter determined if the behavior could be best addressed through SMA or SMP.

3. *Select replacement behavior.* After Lillian and Mr. Peter clearly defined and outlined the target behavior, a new, more desirable, behavior was identified. The desired behavior was equally descriptive and its development involved Lillian's input, increasing her motivation to make strides toward meeting the goal of the replacement behavior. It was imperative that the replacement behavior serve the same purpose for Lillian as the initial behavior of concern.

   In Mr. Peter's class, Lillian was frequently out of her seat, attempting to engage her peers in conversation. Upon careful collection of data, and discussions with Lillian, Mr. Peter was able to conclude that the purpose of her behavior was to seek attention from her peers, particularly because she was uninterested in mathematics. Consequently, Mr. Peter needed to develop a replacement behavior that satisfied Lillian's attention-seeking needs.

Rather than moving about the classroom distracting peers, Mr. Peter developed opportunities for Lillian to receive her peers' attention in a more structured and less disruptive manner, contingent upon completing her math assignments. When implementing the self-management strategy, it was critical to ensure that the same needs were being met as the behaviors of concern. Otherwise, Lillian might have lost interest or find the process to be without value or importance.

4. *Determine self-monitoring system.* Just as data may be collected through one of several data management techniques, the self-monitoring system taught to students as a way to assess progress toward goals may vary. Mr. Peter's self-monitoring system appropriately matched the goals as outlined in the replacement behaviors, yet, they were also simple and straightforward enough for Lillian to use.

Consequently, the most effective, yet parsimonious, way for Lillian to record her out-of-seat versus positive attention-seeking behavior was event recording. The data collection tool required Lillian to tally the number of behaviors displayed. Mr. Peter not only carefully assessed the most appropriate self-monitoring system, but also worked with Lillian to ensure that she thoroughly understood the process, including the importance of accurate data collection as it related to making change and achieving goals.

5. *Set goals.* Mr. Peter and Lillian developed goals utilizing the data collected when identifying the behavior of concern and the way that it manifested in the classroom setting. Jointly, both teacher and student found an agreeable goal that was achievable and realistic. Although Lillian may have aimed higher or lower than appropriate, it was her teacher's role to facilitate the goal setting so that she could achieve success with an obtainable goal while challenging herself to make improvements.

Reasonable goals could have been developed according to an increase or decrease by a percentage or by total number. For Lillian, a goal of decreasing her out of seat behavior by 25 percent was appropriate, reasonable, and achievable. Additionally, Lillian and Mr. Peter agreed to target a 10 percent increase for positive opportunities to gain peer attention. For Lillian, 10 percent was a challenge, but deemed appropriate based on her needs.

6. *Implement system.* After defining a clear method of self-monitoring and setting a mutually agreed upon goal, Lillian began to self-monitor her behavioral progress. Initially, discrepancies between actual data and recorded data were anticipated and expected. Lillian's self-monitoring was somewhat inaccurate and Mr. Peter used these opportu-

nities to reteach and enhance her awareness of the behavior of concern.

With additional coaching and support, Lillian was able to accurately record her behaviors with precision. Although it was not the case with Mr. Peter and Lillian, self-monitoring systems may need to be reevaluated and adjusted as the process gets underway.

7. *Evaluate progress.* After initial implementation concerns were addressed, Lillian began using her self-monitoring system on a regular and consistent basis with success. After approximately five weeks, Lillian was meeting her target goals of decreasing her behavior of concern 30 percent of the time and increasing her positive attention seeking behaviors 11 percent of the time.

   If self-monitoring had proven to be challenging based on established goals, Lillian and Mr. Peter would have met again to assess where the system was failing and review goals. This reassessment would have been conducted cautiously and changes would have been made only after a sufficient implementation period.

8. *Increase goals.* After consistent mastery of a goal, Lillian and Mr. Peter met to discuss progress. After decreasing negative behaviors and increasing positive behaviors, new incremental goals were set. Although decreasing negative behaviors had been quite successful for Lillian, she continued to struggle with increasing positive behaviors.

   Her new goals, as decided upon by both Mr. Peter and Lillian, focused on a greater increase in reducing negative behaviors (50 percent from baseline) and only a slight increase in increasing positive behaviors (15 percent from baseline). It was important for Lillian to continue experiencing success, while being challenged to make improvements through her self-monitoring.

9. *Praise generously.* While Lillian had a number of interests, and, like most adolescents, enjoyed tangible rewards, Mr. Peter made a conscious decision to initially avoid using tangibles with Lillian's self-monitoring plan. For many students, including Lillian, the act of self-monitoring and positive praise and reinforcement can be enough to motivate and increase student engagement. Providing tangible rewards for self-monitoring should be done with caution and should not be included in initial planning stages unless it is clear that social reinforcers like praise will be ineffective for the target student.

   As with Lillian, the intrinsic reward of positive attention from her peers and adults was sufficient to change her behavior, thus negating concerns from other teachers that praise alone would not be enough to alter Lillian's behavior. Because Mr. Peter consistently and routinely praised Lillian for her progress, tangibles were never a necessary component of her plan.

10. *Evaluate and increase goals.* Just as Mr. Peter and Lillian did during previous self-monitoring stages, they met several more times over the course of the school year to assess and increase goals. This process continued until Lillian independently monitored her behavioral choices. As Lillian successfully completed eighth grade, Mr. Peter shared Lillian's plan with high school teachers and provided a synopsis of progress to date, needed supports, and an outline on how to facilitate an effective transition to high school.

LILLIAN'S TRANSITION TO HIGH SCHOOL

Through the systematic use of a self-monitoring system, Lillian developed the necessary skills for academic and social success at Campbell Middle School. She is on her way to enhancing her self-management skills, ultimately translating into self-regulation of behavior. Self-monitoring proved to be a valuable tool for Lillian that assisted with the transition from middle to high school. Lillian and her team are now working to systematically decrease the need for self-monitoring sheets and are working to have her periodically check in with a system, to ensure that her success continues.

Her self-monitoring skills will ultimately help foster the acquisition of qualifications necessary for graduation and employment. While there were challenges that arose along the way, Lillian's teachers reviewed and made adjustments in the goals to support Lillian. It is imperative that educators, like Lillian's team, identify students who are in need of additional supports and thoughtfully provide positive interventions to ensure student success.

REFERENCES

Agran, M., King-Sears, M. E., Wehmeyer, M. L., & Copeland, S. R. (2003). *Student-directed learning.* Baltimore, MD: Paul H. Brookes.

Brigham, F. J., & Brigham, M. S. P. (2010). Preventive instruction: Response to intervention can catch students before their problems become insurmountable. *The American School Board Journal, 197*(6), 32–33.

Ganz, J. B. (2008). Self-monitoring across age and ability levels: Teaching students to implement their own positive behavioral interventions. *Preventing School Failure, 53,* 39–48.

Hott, B. L., & Walker, J. D. (February/April 2012). Five tips to increase student participation in the secondary classroom. *Learning Disabilities Forum,* pp. 7–11. Retrieved from http://www.cldinternational.org/Journals/LDForum/LDF_2012_FebAprfinal_web.pdf

Ingram, K., Lewis-Palmer, T., & Sugai, G. (2005). Comparing the effectiveness of function-based and non-function-based intervention plans. *Journal of Positive Behavioral Interventions, 7,* 224–226.

Kauffman, J. M., & Brigham, F. J. (2009). *Working with troubled children.* Verona, WI: Full Court Press.

King-Sears, M. E. (2008). Using teacher and researcher data to evaluate the effects of self-management in an inclusive classroom. *Preventing School Failure, 52,* 25–34.

Kitsantas, A., & Zimmerman, B. J. (2009). College students' homework and academic achievement: The mediating role of self-regulatory beliefs. *Metacognition Learning, 4,* 145–156.

Sheffield, K., & Waller, R. J. (2010). A review of single-case studies utilizing self-monitoring interventions to reduce problem classroom behaviors. *Beyond Behavior, 19,* 7–13.

Zimmerman, B. J. (2008). Investigating self-regulation and motivation: Historical background, methodological developments, and future prospects. *American Educational Research Journal, 45,* 166–183.

Chapter Four

Schoolize or Culturalize "Them" Within our Classroom Community

Hillary Merk

RIGHT VERSUS WRONG BEHAVIOR: WHO DECIDES?

"It's time to get ready for the day, second graders. Please find a place in the classroom and begin moving your bodies and dancing to the music." This is a typical morning routine for students in this large urban K–8 school; this activity allows students to get warmed up and mentally and physically prepared for the school day.

Three students (all boys, all African American) are dancing around in a small group, while the rest of the students dance in their own space and keep to themselves. In fact, some students standing in their own space are not dancing or moving at all, but remain quiet and off the teacher's radar. During this movement/warm-up activity, the teacher continues to closely monitor the African American boys, separating them multiple times.

These boys are moving in a way that somewhat mimics what can be seen in hip-hop videos, nothing graphic or sexual, but definitely not what the rest of the students are doing. They are moving around (dancing), which is required of all students by the teacher. She intervenes and separates them three times during the movement activity in an attempt to stop this (mis?)behavior from happening. The teacher comments, "It's amazing how cliquey they already are, isn't it?"

These students were following the teacher's directions as they were dancing to the music and warming up for the day. However, the *clique* (the group of African American boys) was demonstrating dance moves that were possibly unfamiliar to the White middle-class female teacher, and/or were (mis)understood as being *inappropriate*. These students were not mimicking

27

the teacher's dance moves, like many other White students, who were praised for doing the right thing. Instead, they were dancing in a way that was familiar to them, which appeared to be a moment when these students were self-regulating but apparently not to the standards of the *right* school behaviors.

The students do not *choose* to dance and move around the room like the other White students—and because "whiteness is a marker for a location of social privilege" (Maher & Tetreault, 1998, p. 139) their behavior is quickly modified.

The *right* behavior is synonymous with *normal* behavior, which represents White ways of being. Thus, "whiteness, like maleness, becomes the norm for 'human,' the basis for universality and detachment; it is the often silent and invisible basis against which other racial and cultural identities are named as "Other" (Maher & Tetreault, 1998, p. 139). Thus, classroom management incidents may arise more frequently in classroom where teachers and students do not share similar backgrounds, such as languages, ethnicities, and experiences (Milner & Tenore, 2010).

What is necessary, then, is an understanding of the context and of those who make up the learning environment, including the teachers reflecting on their own background and the role that their background plays in their classroom management decisions. This in-depth exploration of those who make up the learning environment would allow teachers to be responsive to their students needs, permitting equity in the classroom.

SCHOOLIZE OR CULTURALIZE "THEM"

Having discussions around the role that race, class, and gender play in classroom management is integral to becoming culturally responsive classroom managers (Weinstein, Tomlinson-Clarke, & Curran, 2004). Thus, reflecting on one's varied responses to behavior in the classroom is a place to start; focusing on "who is being disciplined the most and why?" As Ravitch (2010) stated, "it is doubt that shows we are still thinking, still willing to reexamine hardened beliefs when confronted with new facts and new evidence" (p. 2).

> Sometimes I think a lot of the discipline rates have to do with the achievement gap. You know boys do not achieve quite as well in schools, anyway so then you add on the African American discrepancy too and they get even more frustrated and use more attention getting behavior to get out of work or whatever. (Second grade teacher)

In classrooms such as this, the disproportionate discipline rates (see for instance, Milner & Tenore, 2010) are often attributed to low achieving boys, and to the racial stereotype that African American boys employ more attention-getting behaviors so they may get out of work. Therefore, in order for the students to demonstrate the *right* behavior, some teachers believe they have to "kind of culturalize them for schools, or schoolize them or something like that of the expectations because a lot of them don't have those at home*"* (Second grade teacher).

However, only certain groups, or clientele, need to be culturalized or schoolized. What is problematic about this code language is that it often means students of color and those from low socioeconomic backgrounds.

> I work really really hard to help kids learn to not do things immediately just because they feel like it, well that and also violence . . . to not solve their problems with violence. That is kind of like our whole school goal. We try to work really hard against that. In my classroom though, I just try really hard to teach kids to use other skills and sometimes have to teach them those skills. (Second grade teacher)

These teachers believe that because the students do not have the structure at home, *they* are at fault for misbehavior, not the structures of schooling. It is assumed that the misbehavior lies innately in the student; thus, external control is always necessary. The problem is often placed on the child and based on the student's ascribed characteristics; these *natural* characteristics often require teachers to directly teach students to display the *right* school behaviors. However, when teachers respond and how they respond can often vary from student to student.

At one end of the continuum is an immediate response such as an exit from the group or classroom, and at the opposite end is a complete overlooking of the (mis?)behavior. Consistency is a key term used throughout the classroom management research (Freiberg, 1999), but it does not always translate into practice.

BREAKING THE MOLD

It appears that because there is a discursive shift in classroom management literature from classroom discipline to classroom management to classroom community (Jones & Jones, 2013), there is also an ideological shift. The community framework emphasizes that teachers work *with students* to create classroom expectations, talk about student behavior within a community or teamwork framework, and work together to solve classroom incidents (Wolk, 2003).

Teachers emphasize the importance of students caring for one another and treating each other with kindness as key elements to a successful community approach to classroom management. "I try to tell them that if they just treat each other with kindness and care about each other then all the other stuff kind of falls into place" (Second grade teacher). Again, it is the students' *choice* to treat each other with kindness; however, certain clientele who need to be culturalized do not actually get to make that choice.

What appears to be lacking from this community-building framework for classroom management is a critical analysis of what the right behavior is and the approaches teachers use to guide students toward the desired classroom behavior. The *right* school behaviors were moments when students received praise for behaviors, such as knowing where the learning is by:

• looking at the teacher,
• self-regulating during center time so the teacher can actually teach,
• raising a hand to speak, and
• demonstrating an overall ability to demonstrate intrinsic self-control of behavior.

Thus, Whiteness is the "dominating conceptual apparatus" (Maher & Tetreault, 1998, p. 145) for these approaches, as these behaviors emulate a White middle-class way of being.

There is little conflict and minimal, if any, discussion of *why* certain behaviors are deemed the *right* behavior. The age-old "because I say so" philosophy applies to most situations. Therefore, the teacher has few one-on-one behavioral interventions or confrontations with students, especially when students are able to demonstrate the *right* school behaviors. Moreover, direct confrontation is often avoided by dismissing the student from the room altogether.

Although there has been an attempt to situate classroom management within the changing demographics of schools, the community-building framework (Jones & Jones, 2013) overwhelmingly receives the most attention from teachers for its comfortable language and user-friendly, practical methods. This framework allows for statements such as "it's not about race, it's more about respect and responsibility within our classroom community." However, this seems to be an inadequate response to address the disproportionate discipline rates; such discourse obscures issues of race rather than addressing them openly.

Carter (1998) argued that civil discourse, such as the community-building framework, minimizes conflict *and* diversity by repressing public discussions of race and/or masking the conversations under code words. The silences around the role of race in classroom management practices often accompanies inaction to address the racial inequities in discipline (Mayo, 2002). Thus, by suppressing conflict and focusing on helping students get along with one another, educators have focused on attitudinal approaches to ending biases in their classroom management practices, rather than attending to social, political, and economic critique (Mayo).

CONCLUSION

"The search for good or bad intentions is a misleading diversion from the tasks of transforming public education. Intentions must be directed toward the disruption of what is and what appears inevitable, not toward well-meaning compliance" (Fine, 1991, p. 183). As the demographics of schools are rapidly changing (Ladson-Billings, 2005), and the disproportionate discipline rates are present in schools across the United States (Gordon, 1998; Mrozowksi, 2002), it becomes clear that the interrogation of race is needed within dominant classroom management ideology in general, and the community-building framework specifically.

This discourse serves as an extension to the culturally responsive literature (Gay, 2002; Weinstein et al., 2004) by infusing a critical theoretical perspective of race into the field of classroom management. Additionally, in order to identify and critique how hegemonic dominant ideology, social stratification, and power influence teachers' classroom management understandings and practices, as well as students' academic and behavioral outcomes, a more critical discussion of classroom management should begin in an effort to eliminate the disproportionate discipline rates.

As educators, we should take our own professional work and critically explore how we teach and how our own identity and ideological framework impact our teaching. Having colleagues observe lessons that specifically attend to the areas of inequitable discipline would allow teachers to see what may be invisible to them.

Increased staff developments in schools today regarding critical discussions of classroom management and school-wide management plans are crucial as well. "The very experience of struggling together in conversations to understand and attack racial inequality [is] itself an essential outcome of 'talking about race'" (Pollock, 2004, p. 221).

Dominant classroom management ideology situates the misbehavior innately in the child. The responsibility for behavior problems remains in the *child* and/or family, whereas schools are often given responsibility for academic achievement. If *all students* have to take the state-mandated tests, would not academic achievement levels increase if *all students* were actively engaging in a *meaningful* learning environment? This requires teachers to challenge dominant classroom management discourses and practices; the following examples highlight classroom practices that do just that.

> You know my classroom management plan always mentions that the kids make the rules at the beginning of the year . . . not rules, but we call it, you know, the way we want our class to be . . . class expectations. It mentions my working with students in my philosophy, not working at them or to them. (Second grade teacher)

You know, I won't just say "no I don't want you to, so you won't." We talked it [the option of students sitting in chairs during carpet time] over and we agreed to try it. Just the fact that they wanted to and had been allowed to try it, as opposed to me just saying "no" was so huge. So those kinds of times when they can really sort of make a decision and discovery together, as opposed to me just being the boss person. Not "this will be the way it is because I am older, I am the one with the red pen" or whatever. (Second grade teacher)

Establishing and supporting positive student and teacher interactions in order to foster a meaningful learning community should be the foundation to any classroom management philosophy; after all "the importance of classroom community has become so accepted that it would be difficult to find anyone to persuasively argue against its importance" (Watson & Battistich, 2006, p. 253).

While teacher-student relationships are crucial in the classroom, holding all students to high academic and behavioral expectations and making learning meaningful to every student are essential to an equitable classroom environment as well (Bondy, Ross, Gallingane, & Hambacher, 2007).

To achieve this essential goal, organization, structure, and behavior expectations are needed in all classrooms in order for students to engage in the learning; the tactic to obtain that structure must begin with an understanding of what and whose purpose the order is serving. Thus, this critical classroom management discussion works to disrupt the foundation on which dominant classroom management approaches rest.

Continued dialogue should take place that addresses the following: What and whose purpose does dominant classroom management ideology serve? Who benefits and how? And, what culturally responsive classroom management strategies help increase academic learning gains?

REFERENCES

Bondy, E., Ross, D. D., Gallingane, C., & Hambacher, E. (2007). Creating environments of success and resilience. *Urban Education, 42,* 326–348.

Carter, S. (1998). *Civility: Manners, morals, and the etiquette of democracy.* New York, NY: Basic Books.

Fine, M. (1991). *Framing dropouts: Notes on the politics of urban public high school.* Albany, NY: State University of New York.

Freiberg, H. J. (1999). Consistency management and cooperative discipline: From tourists to citizens in the classroom. In H. J. Freiberg (Ed.), *Beyond behaviorism: Changing the classroom management paradigm* (pp. 75–97). Boston, MA: Allyn & Bacon.

Gay, G. (2002). Preparing for culturally responsive teaching. *Journal of Teacher Education, 53,* 106–123.

Gordon, R. (1998). *Education and race: A journalist's handbook.* Oakland, CA: Applied Research Center.

Jones, V., & Jones, L. (2013). *Comprehensive classroom management: Creating communities of support and solving problems.* (10th ed.). Upper Saddle River, NJ: Pearson.

Ladson-Billings, G. J. (2005). Is the team all right? Diversity and teacher education. *Journal of Teacher Education, 56,* 229–234.

Maher, F., & Tetreault, M. K. T. (1998). "They got the paradigm and painted it white": Whiteness and pedagogies of positionality. In J. L. Kincheloe, S. R. Steinberg, N. M. Rodriguez, & R. E. Chennault (Eds.), *White reign: Deploying whiteness in America* (pp.138–158). New York, NY: St. Martin's Press.

Mayo, C. (2002). The binds that tie: Civility and social difference. *Educational Theory, 52,* 169–187.

Milner, R. H., & Tenore, F. B. (2010). Classroom management in diverse classrooms. *Urban Education, 45,* 560–603.

Mrozowksi, J. (2002, March 12). Suspension rate higher for black pupils here: Out of proportion to population. *The Cincinnati Enquirer,* Retrieved from http://enquirer.com/editions/2002/03/12/loc_suspension_rate.html

Pollock, M. (2004). *Colormute: Race talk dilemmas in an American school.* Princeton, NJ: Princeton University Press.

Ravitch, D. (2010). *The death and life of the great American school system: How testing and choice are undermining education.* New York, NY: Basic Books.

Watson, M., & Battistich, V. (2006). Building and sustaining caring communities. In C. M. Everston & C. S. Weinstein (Eds.), *Handbook of classroom management: Research, practice, and contemporary issues* (pp. 253–279)*.* Mahwah, NJ: Lawrence Erlbaum.

Weinstein, C. S., Tomlinson-Clarke, S., & Curran, M. (2004). Toward a conception of culturally responsive classroom management. *Journal of Teacher Education, 55,* 25–38.

Wolk, S. (2003). Hearts and minds. *Educational Leadership, 61*(1), 14–18.

Chapter Five

Classroom Management in the Corridor: Teacher-Student Negotiations of an Educational Authority Relationship Outside of the Classroom Context

Anneli Frelin

Lisa was a troubled, sad, and perhaps even depressed, high school girl. She would simply hang around the school, and did not want to attend classes. When she told Adrian, her math teacher,* that she could do her work outside the classroom instead of in class, Adrian decided to agree to her proposal. When Adrian reflected on how he handled Lisa's resistance to attend his class, he said that forcing her to attend would have done more damage than good. Rather than debate the issue of Lisa's class attendance, he waited until he thought the timing was right, and then would join her occasionally in the corridor and start a casual conversation.

During these encounters, he would avoid talking about math, and instead chat casually, listen, and have a laugh or two and then leave. Sometimes his parting words would be of the kind that made Lisa think: "Well, he is . . . human." Beyond the intention of casually slipping into talks with Lisa and getting a feel for the situation, Adrian had no master plan with regard to how the conversation should go. He just tried to find out what worked in making contact while not pushing too hard.

Their corridor talks were part of an overall strategy of involvement in a positive, informal interaction with Lisa, which was disconnected from the subject matter, but aimed at building a closer, more trusting relationship. Adrian considered two aspects of their relationship: first, Lisa's passing the math course, and secondly, her growing as a person and developing into a good human being. In his view, if Lisa could come to the point of regarding him as a good person who wished her well, this would motivate and inspire her to do well and come to his class.

One day, after their corridor talks had continued for some time, Lisa entered the doorway of Adrian's classroom—an event that he was careful not to mark with a great deal of fanfare:

> If I walk up to her and exclaim, "How nice of you to come, that's great!" then she'll just turn around and walk out, thinking: "I don't want everyone to notice me, watching me come in." It probably takes a huge effort to come into the classroom like that. I can even sense her thinking: "Do Not Talk To Me. Say Nothing to me. Leave me alone. I promise to sit here and try to do something." (Frelin, 2010, p. 121)

Even after Lisa began attending Adrian's math classes, he continued to maintain the corridor talks and to build upon the positive trustful relationship that had developed between them. During class, he also made sure that the tasks that he gave Lisa were reasonable and varied. She continued to attend his class and began to ask questions; gradually her mood improved.

Later on, Lisa brought Adrian an old practice test with a request for more such practice problems, which he interpreted as an expression of Lisa's will to learn and succeed. Lisa was eventually able to pass math. Looking back and remembering how, at the start, Lisa almost swore at him on sight, Adrian felt good about this development.

RELATIONAL PRACTICES GUIDED BY A WIDE TASK PERCEPTION

Adrian's relational practices, featured in the above referenced story, are motivated by a specific *task perception* (Kelchtermans, 1993). The practices by which Adrian seeks to improve the quality of the student-teacher relationship are intended to promote several end results at once. They range from more narrow goals (such as subject matter learning or making passing grades) to broader ones (such as fostering democratic citizenship or furthering human progress in general).

As a teacher, Adrian's pedagogy is guided by a value judgment that provides him with a strong incentive for helping his students. In order to do so, he attempts to find the time to have personal talks with them, preferably one on one. He views these conversations as a means of building a trusting relationship, so that his students consider Adrian to be a just person who wishes them well. The talks involve listening to the student, and taking seriously whatever he or she has to say.

Class time is generally quite busy, and thus, most of these personal inter-actions take place at other times. Adrian says that he mostly uses part of the time he would otherwise spend on lesson planning. Nonetheless, he deliber-ately prioritizes by spending time in the corridors, assumes that this is valu-able, and concludes that the students appreciate it, too. The practice of inter-acting informally outside of the classroom situation, through personal talks, listening, and by using praise, are all means by which Adrian establishes and maintains *educational relationships* (Frelin, 2010, 2013) with individual stu-dents.

AUTHORITY AS A RELATIONAL AND DYNAMIC PHENOMENON

Adrian's corridor talks can be framed in terms of a teacher's relational prac-tices of negotiating a relationship of authority with individual students. Pace and Hemmings's (2006) as well as Burbules's (1993) work on authority provide tools for analyzing such negotiations. Authority can be viewed as the probability by which a person gains voluntary obedience from others, which in turn rests on others' belief in the *legitimacy* of her or his actions. Pace and Hemmings (2006), inspired by Weber, described four ideal types of author-ity, which have different sources of legitimacy for teachers:

1. *Traditional authority,* based on the longstanding tradition of giving superior status to teachers just because they inhabit that role;
2. *Charismatic authority,* based on a teacher's exceptional qualities and ability to evoke emotional attachment and commitment from students;
3. *Legal-rational or bureaucratic authority,* based on rules and policies, but sometimes dependent on power (e.g., the ability to use rewards or punishments), which suggest that compliance is not voluntary; and
4. *Professional authority,* based on the legitimacy of teachers' expert knowledge and/or pedagogical skills.

As Pace and Hemmings (2006) observed, the notion of teachers' classroom authority as a dynamic social construction is "jointly negotiated through the symbolic actions of teachers and students and [. . .] shaped by local contex-tual forces and larger social, political, and cultural factors" (p. 1), and as such, it is internally and externally influenced. Such authority is dependent on students' consent to the teacher's legitimacy and a shared moral order, and is enacted through students and teachers engaging in dynamic negotia-tions in open or subtle forms.

Hence, the space available for such teacher-student negotiations varies depending on the interaction and relation between the teacher and student, whose actions can open and close opportunities for negotiations, as well as the larger context in which they are situated (Frelin & Grannäs, 2010). For example, at this school, Adrian had the option to let Lisa temporarily sit in the corridor during his lesson without either of them being punished by the school management. Had the rules been stricter, this space would not have existed.

Those who are involved in an intersubjective relation of authority are placed within certain social circumstances but are also in a position to make choices and act within that relation in different ways (Bingham, 2004). The student, thus, has the agency to accept or reject the authority of the teacher as someone who has something to offer the student. Bingham emphasized that the content of education is, itself, not disconnected from this relation; the student can decide to accept or reject the content the teacher offers as well as the teacher.

The possibility for implementing curriculum, then, can be viewed as emerging within a relation between teacher and student although the student *could* make the choice to accept the content while rejecting the teacher. Pace's (2003) ethnographic study showed, on the classroom level, how authority-as-hybrids—consisting of different kinds of authority relationships—are the result of teachers' and students' negotiation of their agendas in a context of conflicting demands.

Pace (2003) discussed the problem of hybridized authority relations, where teachers' directives and underpinnings are unclear. In these authority relations, teachers draw on a combination of orientations, which may create ambiguous messages, which undercut the significance of the subject matter.

By building on Pace's (2003) argument, one may conclude that hybridized authority relations may be indications of a mismatch between the bases of legitimacy claimed by the teacher and the students. In other words, the use of bureaucratic authority in relation to a student, such as threatening her or him with a bad grade if work is not done, is problematic when the student resists this kind of authority but responds to charismatic authority instead.

TEACHER-STUDENT NEGOTIATION OF AN EDUCATIONAL AUTHORITY RELATIONSHIP

Adrian's story may be framed as a negotiation of an authority relationship, where different bases of legitimacy are in play. Most negotiations of authority relationships between students and teachers are very subtle and require very little attention. Lisa does not act like most students, and the practice in which Adrian engages is rather demanding. In the situation where Lisa refused to participate in his math class, Adrian made the judgment that confrontation or coercion—although it may have resulted in nonconsensual obedience—was not an appropriate means of inducing her to participate, and thus not an effective means of fulfilling the educational ends he sought.

Lisa's refusal to participate could indicate that she did not consider his claims to authority legitimate just because his position was that as a teacher. In other words, she made it clear that a traditional authority relationship could not be established. Since neither getting a good grade nor the intrinsic motivation of learning seemed important enough to her, bureaucratic or professional bases of legitimacy, such as Adrian's subject matter knowledge, could not be used by him.

In an effort to engage Lisa, Adrian had to commit to establishing some kind of relationship with her, which he judged could be accomplished through interaction with her in the only place she agreed to—the corridor. It also was a place where negotiations could be conducted privately, one on one, and not before the rest of the class.

By departing from the position of teacher, which Lisa refused in terms of both space and manner, Adrian's actions can be interpreted as the initiation of a negotiation of authority. He conveyed to Lisa that he was not claiming any of the bases of legitimacy that she resisted, but wanted to enter into a relation of dialogue with her. Adrian claims that he did not enter with any fixed strategies or agendas; he resisted the interpretation that the talks in the corridor were aimed directly at getting Lisa to come to his classes.

Further, Adrian's attitude indicates that his primary end was to establish the relationship in itself, which shows that their relationship was not dependent on math learning, but on a state of being in dialogue. That, in itself, constituted the enactment of an end, and which indirectly could result in achieving other ends as well. According to Nucci (2006), teacher practices by which students experience *goodwill* during their time in school are important for students' moral and social growth. One of Adrian's aims was to establish trust, and he saw Lisa's trust—her growing view of him as a benevolent and just person—as something that would continue to develop over time.

As students sometimes experience teachers' actions as violating their trust, trust can also be built on the absence of violation. Adrian describes Lisa's first entrance into the classroom as a vulnerable situation that called upon him to be very aware of his reactions, and not express the joy he felt inside. If he had made a public display of his emotions, this would have drawn attention to Lisa's situation in front of the class, which might have caused Lisa to feel as if her trust had been violated. Students also can experience teachers' incorrect or distrustful perceptions of them, or lack of benevolence, as violations that cause damage to trustful relations.

Lisa's entrance into the classroom can be interpreted as an act of negotiation, in which she gives up her resistance by extending the already established relationship with Adrian to the classroom, and to the practice of learning math. This would make her relationship with the teacher connected to her relation with the content he offers, as suggested by Bingham (2004).

If one assumes that her trust in Adrian was built from interaction, which was dependent to some degree on the fact that he listened to her, recognized her as a person, and showed concern for her, this interaction constituted a *dialogical* basis of legitimacy (Burbules, 1993) for authority in their relationship.

CONCLUSION

By drawing on Pace and Hemmings (2006), we see that teacher authority is viewed as relational, negotiated, dynamic, and subject to various influences. Establishing student trust as a basis for professional authority relationships also means that loss of trust may result in loss of authority. Additionally, it might mean that the dynamics of relationships render them constantly open to renegotiation. However, the negotiations begin at some point.

After this opening encounter, because the process of interaction continuously shapes the relationship, the previous practice constitutes the starting point for the next negotiation. The practice of building trust constitutes a relational basis from which the teachers' actions are interpreted by students in new situations.

While Adrian's interaction with students mostly takes place within the classroom, meeting students in spaces that are outside this context—such as corridors—provides opportunities for informal interaction that can contribute to a positive relationship (van Tartwijk, den Brok, Veldman, & Wubbels, 2009). Through negotiations, different bases of legitimacy are claimed. Adrian's task perception, thus, transforms the corridor into an important alternate work space.

In situations like these, negotiating a relationship in which it is possible to rely upon dialogical legitimacy as a basis for authority can be a precondition for being able to negotiate other bases for authority such as the professional (e.g., expert knowledge in math). Hence, classroom management and student engagement sometimes start in the corridor.

*Teachers in Sweden are customarily addressed by their first names.

REFERENCES

Bingham, C. W. (2004). Let's treat authority relationally. In C. W. Bingham & A. M. Sidorkin (Eds.), *No education without relation* (pp. 23–38). New York, NY: Peter Lang.

Burbules, N. C. (1993). *Dialogue in teaching: Theory and practice.* New York, NY: Teachers College Press.

Frelin, A. (2010). *Teachers' relational practices and professionality.* (Unpublished doctoral dissertation). Uppsala University, Uppsala, Sweden.

Frelin, A. (2013). *Exploring teachers' relational professionalism in schools.* Rotterdam, The Netherlands: Sense Publishers.

Frelin, A., & Grannäs, J. (2010). Negotiations left behind: In-between spaces of teacher-student negotiation and their significance for education. *Journal of Curriculum Studies, 42,* 353–369.

Kelchtermans, G. (1993). Getting the story, understanding the lives: From career stories to teachers' professional development. *Teaching and Teacher Education, 9,* 443–456.

Nucci, L. (2006). Classroom management for moral and social development. In C. M. Evertson & C. S. Weinstein (Eds.), *Handbook of classroom management: Research, practice, and contemporary issues* (pp. 711–731). Mahwah, NJ: Lawrence Erlbaum.

Pace, J. L. (2003). Revisiting classroom authority: Theory and ideology meet practice. *Teachers College Record, 105,* 1559–1585.

Pace, J. L., & Hemmings, A. (2006). *Classroom authority: Theory, research, and practice.* Mahwah, NJ: Lawrence Erlbaum.

van Tartwijk, J., den Brok, P., Veldman, I., & Wubbels, T. (2009). Teachers' practical knowledge about classroom management in multicultural classrooms. *Teaching and Teacher Education, 25,* 453–460.

Chapter Six

I'm Not a Reluctant Learner! I Just Need a Chance to Connect and Do Well in School

Lou Denti

MOTIVATING STUDENTS: MORE COMPLEX THAN ONE THINKS

Students nowadays bring a host of complicated and complex emotional issues with them to the schoolhouse door each and every day. Sadly, many teachers are woefully unprepared to deal with the exigencies of students with social challenges. As a result, teacher criticisms abound, such as, "I don't have the time to deal with students who are unmotivated. . . . Kids today are lazy and don't want to learn. . . . They all seem like ADD [attention deficit disorder] . . . and . . . Parents really don't care."

These negative impressions of students offer little in the way of finding and applying proactive solutions. However, discovering unique approaches and constructive language to empower students boosts teacher confidence and effectiveness. The following three case vignettes explicate the ways teachers can set up an environment that is motivating and engaging. Moreover, students can develop the mindset and skills that offer them a chance to be successful in school.

MOTIVATING MIDDLE SCHOOLER JOHNNY: TAKING THE LONG VIEW

Jonathan, a seventh grader in an upscale middle school, very rarely participates in class, appears disengaged, or retreats into his own world most of the time. The teacher, Mrs. Tangerly, has made overtures to encourage Jonathan by moving him to the front of the classroom and by giving him extra time to do his work. Jonathan's disinterested behavior and nonresponsiveness to her overtures have led Mrs. Tangerly to stop offering him assistance.

Instead, she avoids him and only talks to him when issuing a directive such as staying on task or imploring him to finish his work in a timely fashion. Jonathan's classmates have dubbed him the "slacker dude," from the character Jeff Spicoli in the movie *Fast Times at Ridgemont High* (Linson, Izoff, & Heckerling, 1982), who was the ultimate goof-off.

The students in his class, like their teacher, have written him off as lazy. Jonathan does have a group of friends he hangs out with at break, during lunch, and after school. They are a fringe group with interests ranging from video games to offbeat dressing styles to headbanger music.

Jonathan feels accepted by this group and respected for his juggling ability and card tricks. His closest friends know that his mom and dad went through an acrimonious divorce last year, and Jonathan has been bouncing around from his grandparents' house to his maternal aunt's home to couch surfing periodically at some of his friends' houses.

So how does a teacher who has made an attempt to involve Jonathan continue to offer assistance? First and foremost, the teacher must acknowledge that Jonathan is not unmotivated or reluctant to learn. He is just unmotivated to do what the teacher wants him to do. In his compelling essay "I Won't Learn From You!" Kohl (1992) stated,

> Learning how to not-learn is an intellectual and social challenge; sometimes you have to work very hard at it. It consists of an active, often ingenious, willful rejection of even the most compassionate and well-designed teaching. It subverts attempts at remediation as much as it rejects learning in the first place. (p. 1)

Jonathan is working very hard at not learning. Also, Jonathan's home life has been unsettling and his trust for adults is shaky at best. Another important factor for his teacher to consider revolves around the issue of social comparison. As indicated, Jonathan attends an upscale middle school where social comparison tends to be magnified. Marsh (2005), a prominent educational psychologist, shed some light on what Jonathan might be experiencing.

In their Big-Fish-Little-Pond Effect (BFLPE) model, Marsh and Hau (2003) hypothesized that:

> students compare their own academic ability with the academic abilities of their classmates and use this social comparison impression as one basis for forming their own academic self-concept. A negative BFLPE occurs where equally able students have lower academic self-concepts when they compare themselves to more able students and higher academic self-concepts when they compare themselves with less able students. (pp. 2–3)

Jonathan, though bright, chooses to "slack off" in an effort to maintain a modicum of self-worth. Winning for him becomes a game of not losing the little bit of self-esteem he has at this point in his life. Armed with this knowledge, what strategies could Mrs. Tangerly use to assist Jonathan?

First, Jonathan needs to know that what he cares about is equally as important as what the teacher cares about. When teachers do not understand a student's frustration, they tend to minimize opportunities for active engagement, often ignoring a student who displays nonconforming behaviors. Mrs. Tangerly needs to calibrate what level of effort is required for success in her class, and then create some sort of working agreement with Jonathan so he can begin to obtain that level of success.

Second, Jonathan will only begin to participate when he understands that the teacher trusts in him and he can expect that she will respond to him in a genuine, supportive, and empathetic manner. Greeting Jonathan at the door with a friendly and open salutation, such as "Good to have you in class today, Jonathan" or "Have a great day," creates a positive tone, reinforcing a safe and nonthreatening environment. Making sure that Jonathan receives an "obnoxious" amount of encouragement shows that his teacher cares about him (Denti, 2012).

Third, select a few students who will support Jonathan to get his work done and help him stay on track for in-class and homework assignments. Peer allies who assist Jonathan in developing skills for school success, rather than laughing or encouraging his slacker behavior, will push Jonathan to succeed both socially and academically, thus mitigating the effects of social comparison so prominent in high-performing secondary schools.

Fourth, Jonathan also needs the teacher to offer choices that accent some of his talents. We know that Jonathan has juggling skills, and students on campus respect his ability. By offering Jonathan an opportunity to make some decisions about his education—which might include a class multimedia project, selecting an activity of his choosing, an oral report, or demonstrating something (juggling)—the teacher indicates that he is viewed as a capable learner. As for grading, the teacher might want to consider many opportunities for Jonathan to make up work.

Fifth, self-management is absolutely critical for Jonathan. A written contract wherein Jonathan agrees to monitor his own progress can be most effective. It sends a clear message that his teacher believes in him and his ability to handle himself responsibly.

Last, but not least, the teacher must not give up on Jonathan. She might divide the school year into increments of 60 days and then assess how her relationship with Jonathan is progressing after the first 60-day term. By creating a manageable timeframe, the teacher can then determine if the interventions are working and can make necessary adjustments.

ANGELICA'S ANGST: CHALLENGES AT UPPER ELEMENTARY

Angelica, a fourth grader, gives up easily on all of her academic tasks. Though the teacher prods her to get her work done and has given her numerous opportunities to succeed, she still is falling behind in all of her subjects, especially language arts. She puts her head down on her desk when asked to read out loud telling the teacher she does not feel well.

Recently, Angelica has not been coming to school, complaining of stomachaches and headaches. She does not do her homework on a consistent basis. She often misses key points on her in-class assignments and it appears as if she does not care about her work. Mr. Bronson sends progress notes home each Friday, and Angelica's parents have contacted him on several occasions to find out how they can help at home.

Mr. Bronson has asked his principal for additional counseling assistance for Angelica and has also contacted the resource specialist on campus for suggestions. He has talked to Angelica's third grade teacher to gain a better understanding of Angelica's needs and reviewed her cumulative folder for additional clues.

In his role as teacher, Mr. Bronson is doing everything he can to diagnose Angelica's problems in order to give her the academic assistance she needs. However, as of late, he has been voicing his frustration, telling his colleagues that he has tried everything and she just seems reluctant to learn—she just will not try.

Mr. Bronson, a well-meaning teacher, searches for answers to provide the academic support Angelica requires. After several attempts, his frustration has now led him to believe that Angelica will not even try to learn. Discerning the difference between a student who *won't* (a motivation problem) and a student who *can't* (a skill-based problem) can be perplexing for a teacher who may not have encountered a resistant student like Angelica before. Identifying ways to offer Angelica help can also be puzzling. The following interventions proved successful:

Angelica benefits from a reading and literacy intervention to keep pace with other students in class. Archer and Gleason (1994) introduced a strategy known as RCRC—Read, Cover, Recite, and Check. Angelica reads a paragraph, covers what she read, recites the main ideas back to herself, and then checks to see if she has the gist of the paragraph. She uses this strategy with a partner. The partner, a more capable reader, fills in anything she does not seem to understand. In fact, the whole class could benefit from RCRC, especially when starting a new unit or chapter.

In his book *Building Academic Language,* Zwiers (2008) suggested a strategy known as "comprehend-aloud" where after reading a short passage, students think aloud—to each other in pairs, to the whole class, or both—to gain an understanding of the text. Angelica also profits from a shared reading strategy (Holdaway, 1979).

Shared reading occurs when the teacher and the entire class think through the text together and the teacher prompts students with questions to help them analyze, compare and contrast, interpret, or evaluate what the text or author is trying to convey. These strategies help Angelica process and comprehend information, which makes reading more interesting and enjoyable while de-emphasizing her reading difficulties.

An evidence-based reading intervention targeting comprehension also proves beneficial for Angelica. Her teacher provides similar instruction in his classroom by identifying a few other struggling readers who take advantage of this type of intensive intervention. By offering the strategy for about a half an hour each day for a designated number of weeks, he monitors progress and adjusts instruction accordingly.

Children like Angelica get discouraged after countless failures in school. Mr. Bronson notices a complete change in Angelica's attitude towards reading and literacy once he began to address her identified areas of difficulty. He also notices that what is good for Angelica is invariably good for his entire class. Seeing Angelica prosper from engaging instruction with cogent interventions will help Mr. Bronson determine how to help children who have skill deficits rather than motivational problems.

BRIANNA'S BUSY BRAIN: THE PAIN OF BEING MISUNDERSTOOD

In the third vignette, a young adult named Brianna recounts her experience in second grade some 10 years later. She starts her recollection by saying,

> I had a busy brain and just couldn't pay attention in school. I just stared out the window most of the time. Everything the teacher said went in one ear and out the other ear. His demands for me to stay on task and pay attention would bring me back on task for only a moment, and then I was off daydreaming again. I got in trouble for making paper airplanes out of my assignments and then tossing them across the room.

> I just couldn't sit still and pay attention; my motors needed to be let loose. I just had to get up and move around, talk to others. I knew that I was smart, but I couldn't show it. I made poor grades and was often in trouble. My teacher thought that I didn't want to learn. He would always say if I just paid attention, I could do the work. He gave me extra homework to make up for what I missed in class. I rarely turned in my homework, and when I did, I got big red marks all over the page.

Tearfully, Brianna stated that the teacher did not try to engage her, and that his only recourse was to send her to the office and send notes home to her parents about how poorly she was doing. The teacher told her parents to get *her* counseling and get *her* tested for special education. Her parents, divorced at the time, gave in to his demands and she was placed in special education as learning disabled with the moniker—*reluctant to learn.*

Fortunately, her special education teacher, Mrs. Willows, was kind and caring and found ways for Brianna to learn using her visual and kinesthetic learning styles. She said, to this day, she has to keep busy doing things with her hands and is definitely a visual learner. Now in her first year of community college, she is always asking and answering questions. Her busy brain needs to continue to sort things out to better process information.

Kohn (2006) stated that "we can often predict the way an adult will treat children simply from knowing what she believes about them" (p. 6). In this instance, the second grade teacher believed that something was wrong with Brianna, however, he did little to adjust instruction to accommodate her needs. Instead, he was successful in getting her placed in special education and classified as learning disabled (LD).

Although Brianna was exhibiting the signs of attention deficit disorder (ADD)—impulsivity, inattentiveness, and distractibility—she did not warrant an LD diagnosis and definitely was not reluctant to learn. Osman (1997) pointed out that "every aspect of a child's world can be unsteady when learning is hard" (p. 20).

Learning was definitely hard for Brianna, not because of her lack of intelligence, but because of the inflexibility of the classroom instruction. A classification better suited for Brianna was *dysteachia,* a syndrome wherein the teacher does not provide the necessary learning environment to capitalize on a student's strengths. The following suggestions would have helped Brianna back then and would work equally as well today.

For example, rather than ship Brianna out of the class, the teacher could have provided opportunities for her to move around. He could have scheduled classroom energizers so that all students could get up, stretch, and move to a song or movement routine. The teacher should have immediately moved Brianna to the front of the room and then worked out a signal for on-task behavior. Auditorily saying her name to cue her back on task would have helped her remain actively engaged.

Employing some sort of recording system, such as using tally marks for on-task behavior, would have been most useful for Brianna. She could have kept track of her on-task behavior with tallies issued by the teacher, and the teacher could have kept track on a tally sheet of his own. By simply saying, "Thanks for paying attention, Brianna, give yourself a tally," her attention to the task at hand would have increased.

Recognition for on-task behavior by the teacher was essential for Brianna; recognition by her peers would have been important as well. She should have had multiple opportunities to engage with peer partners and work in cooperative groups.

Providing quality instruction and actively engaging children in school takes tremendous effort, time, persistence, and creativity. Labeling children and then trying to find a place for them tends to create more stress for the teacher and the student. When a child does need extra support from special education or a smaller more intensive learning environment, instruction and behavior support must be done with fidelity.

I'M WORTH THE EXTRA EFFORT FROM MY TEACHERS

Much has been written about reluctant learners, and a host of adjectives or lists usually follow the label. From these three vignettes, one hopefully begins to understand the complexity of working with students who, for one reason or another, find schooling challenging.

If teachers/educators understand that students who resist schooling may *not be motivated to do what you want them to do*, they can then construct an environment to help students grow emotionally and academically. A teacher who encounters this type of learner must be patient; it will take more time for them to develop trust. Once you do gain their trust, they will begin to participate in meaningful ways.

As for students who lack the skills necessary to comprehend academic content, it is incumbent on the teacher to differentiate between a *won't* and a *can't* student. The *won't* student requires motivational strategies; however, the *can't* student calls for teaching and learning strategies to help build skills. They also need encouragement to slowly gain the confidence necessary to succeed in a school's core curriculum.

For students with *busy brains,* a structured learning environment, purposeful hands-on minds-on activities, opportunities to move around, and numerous peer interactive and cooperative groups help these students succeed. A positive, highly structured learning environment coupled with differentiated instruction and recognition for effort creates the context for students with busy brains to succeed both academically and socially.

The three students profiled shed light on the need for teachers to consider viable motivational options for students to thrive in school. By using positive learning supports, the likelihood that students will be more inspired to learn increases (Archer & Hughes, 2011). It also makes students feel respected, giving them a chance to develop their skills and confidence.

Author's Note

All names are pseudonyms.

REFERENCES

Archer, A., & Gleason, M. (1994). *Skills for school success series (Grades 3 – 6)*. Billerica, MA: Curriculum Associates.

Archer, A., & Hughes, C. (2011). *Explicit instruction: Effective and efficient teaching*. New York, NY: Guilford.

Denti, L. (2012). *Proactive classroom management K-8: A practical guide to empower students and teachers*. Thousand Oaks, CA: Corwin Press.

Holdaway, D. (1979). *The foundations of literacy*. Sydney, Australia: Ashton Scholastic.

Kohl, H. (1992). I won't learn from you! Thoughts on the role of assent in learning. *Rethinking Schools, 7*(1), 1–5.

Kohn, A. (2006). *Beyond discipline: From compliance to community*. Alexandria, VA: ASCD.

Linson, A., & Izoff. I. (Producers) & Heckerling, A. (Director). (1982). *Fast times at Ridgemont High* [Motion Picture]. United States: Universal Pictures.

Marsh, H. W. (2005). *Big fish little pond effect on academic self-concept: Cross-cultural and cross-disciplinary generalizability*. Retrieved from http://www.aare.edu.au/05pap/mar05389.pdf

Marsh, H. W., & Hau, K. T. (2003). Big-fish-little-pond effect on academic self-concept: A cross-cultural (26-country) test of the negative effects of academically selective schools. *American Psychologist, 58*, 364–376. doi: 10.1037/0003-066X.58.5.364

Osman, B. B. (1997). *Learning disabilities and ADHD: A family guide to living and learning together*. New York, NY: John Wiley and Sons.

Zwiers, J. (2008). *Building academic language: Essential practices for content classrooms*. San Francisco, CA: Jossey-Bass.

Chapter Seven

Mirrors and Master Switches: Using Interactive Root Metaphors to Support Students' Academic, Social, and Emotional Growth and Development

Terry Murray

THE CHALLENGE

Successfully making the transition from middle school to high school is a daunting challenge for all students. Eighth graders who are moving up to high school may experience both excitement and concern. These students look forward to more freedom, more choices, and new friendships. But they are also nervous, even scared, about being in a new, unfamiliar space with older students. They are anxious about the increased workload and the much harder academic content, as well as concerned about not succeeding.

For students who are struggling academically and beginning to disconnect from their studies and from school, this challenge is even greater. The national statistics that describe the nature of this struggle are sobering. Many at-risk students drop out, often shortly after they enter high school (Editorial Project in Education, 2010; Orfield, 2004; U.S. Department of Education, National Center for Educational Statistics, 2010). Others continue to fall behind and fail to graduate. Nearly one out of every three eighth-grade students in the United States does not graduate from high school, and half of black and Latino students do not graduate (Orfield).

Particularly in light of these statistics, the need to support students in successfully making this transition may also be a disheartening challenge for educators. School districts across the United States have responded to this phenomenon by developing programs to meet the needs of students who are in the midst of academic and life transitions. This chapter describes the efforts of the Crossroads City School District in preparing students for success in the classroom and in life, and their unique approach to addressing the academic, social, and emotional needs of incoming freshmen who have been identified as struggling learners.

Located in southeastern New York, Crossroads is a racially and ethnically diverse community with a population of 16,000. The school district serves 3,800 students. In response to the challenge of supporting *all* of its students in transitioning from middle school to high school, the district administrators, faculty, and staff reflected on two questions:

1. How do we support students in making the transition from middle to high school?
2. What educational tools and processes can be used to effectively address the unique needs of ninth graders who have been identified as struggling learners and who are disconnected from their studies and from their teachers?

A HOLISTIC RESPONSE

Recognizing that the transition between eighth and ninth grade is a defining period for young adult students as well as a critical point for struggling students who are typically behind academically and at risk of dropping out, the Crossroads City School District developed a Freshman Initiative Program. Similar programs have been established across the United States, but they vary widely, from one-day orientations to full school-year curricula. After consideration, the district decided to take a comprehensive approach to respond to this teaching and learning challenge.

As one component of the overall program, the Freshman Seminar was created to provide ongoing support for at-risk students. For a full semester, students met daily for one period. Working with a consultant, the high school staff designed and implemented a holistic curriculum for this seminar. In addition to supporting the development of the students' literacy and study skills, the program was designed to create a safe, caring, participatory learning environment which also fosters the development of social-emotional skills.

The social-emotional component of this district's initiative is grounded in the research conducted by the Collaborative for Academic, Social, and Emotional Learning (CASEL) (Zins & Elias, 2006). As described by CASEL (2011), social-emotional learning (SEL) is "a process for helping children and even adults develop the fundamental skills for life effectiveness. SEL teaches the skills we all need to handle ourselves, our relationships, and our work, effectively and ethically" (p. 1).

Multiple studies have established that the integration of social-emotional programs into the curriculum may have a direct as well as an indirect impact on student learning and school success (Durlak, Weissberg, & Pachan, 2010; Elbertson, Bracket, & Weissberg, 2010; Payton et al., 2008). There is solid evidence demonstrating that creating safe, caring, and participatory learning environments, as well as teaching social-emotional competencies foster greater attachment to school, while also decreasing high-risk behavior and increasing pro-social behavior (CASEL, 2011).

FOCUSING ON THE USE OF METAPHORS FOR ENGAGING STUDENTS

In developing an approach to integrating social-emotional learning into the Freshman Seminar curriculum, the teaching team working with this group of students focused on the use of metaphors in lessons and projects as (a) "mirrors for understanding the challenges [students] are encountering at [this stage in their life]" (Perry & Cooper, 2001, p. 42) and (b) master switches (Tobin, 1990) for helping students understand who they have been and who they want to become.

Botha (2009) described these types of metaphors as *root* and *interactive*. According to Botha, root metaphors are the deepest type of metaphors, grounded in philosophical, mythical, and spiritual traditions. Interactive metaphors are understood as vehicles for developing new world views that can guide people in moving forward in their growth and development.

Media theorist and cultural critic Postman (1996) described these root and interactive metaphors and the processes for engaging students with them as "word weaving" and "world making." He noted that "definitions, questions and metaphors are three of the most potent elements with which human language constructs a world view" (p. 176).

Postman (1996) also observed that, typically, educators do not use metaphors to build awareness and promote growth. Recognizing the power and potential of metaphors for meaningfully engaging students in the Freshman Seminar class, faculty and a consultant designed a sequence of lessons that focused on the interactive root metaphor *journey*.

The concept of journey and the act of journeying are common themes in literature, art, and film. Students read mythology, as well as classical and contemporary stories about people who venture out into the unknown heroically. They also are immersed in a popular culture that explores the journey in music, media, and video games. To support students' deeper understanding of and connection with this metaphor of journey in the Freshman Seminar classes, the students were introduced to lessons that explored labyrinths and mazes, the Heroic Journey Model (Campbell, 1949), and game boards as distinct journey metaphors.

While labyrinths and mazes and the Heroic Journey model draw on deep mythical and archetypal sources, as a metaphor, game boards draw their power from significant childhood memories and from popular culture. Though all three of these journey metaphors provided rich, evocative opportunities for student engagement and social-emotional learning in the Freshman Seminar classes, this chapter focuses on the game board as a metaphor for students' journeys from childhood to adulthood.

MOVING FORWARD, MOVING BACK, AND SOLVING PROBLEMS ALONG THE WAY

The Freshman Seminar teaching team's approach to fostering social-emotional learning was activity and project based. CASEL (2011) research has shown that pedagogical approaches that are experiential, collaborative, and use problem-solving skills have proved particularly effective in developing important intra- and interpersonal skills. The Game Board Project incorporated all of these approaches and over two academic years, five Freshman Seminar classes created game boards.

In preparation for the class work, a progression of blank squares that formed a serpentine path was drawn on a roll of banner paper of approximately 36"x 60" in size. In addition, a spinner for determining how many squares players would move forward and backward was created. The beginning of the path was labeled *childhood* and the end of the path was labeled *adulthood*. Additional supplies assembled included markers, glue sticks, sheets of paper cut to the size of the game board squares, and supplementary sheets of paper labeled with a large exclamation mark and the word *dilemma* on one side of the sheet.

On the day that the Game Board Project was to begin, the blank game board was taped to the board in front of the classroom so that it was visible when the students walked into class. The project was initiated with the following question: "What do you see on the front board?" Students quickly recognized the image as a basic game board. Through further discussion, it was evident that all of the students, even in an era of video games, were familiar with board games, and quickly named versions, including *Chutes and Ladders, Candy Land, Life, Monopoly*, and so on.

Students also readily identified the basic strategies in these games: using a die or spinner to determine the number of squares moved, the dynamic of moving forward and backward on the board in response to situations or scenarios encountered, and the general goal of getting to the end of the path to win the game.

With the game board basics recalled, it was an easy transition to move the class from thinking about game boards to working collaboratively to create a game board. The students were asked to imagine the progression of squares on the blank game board as steps along the route from childhood to adulthood.

Creating this game board meant that they would have to both look back on their life and look ahead to their near future. In describing the task, the students were given choices: they could work individually or in pairs or triads, and they could either create scenarios to place in the squares on the game board, or they could create dilemma cards. Many students ended up creating both squares and dilemmas.

In each game square, the students described an experience that might occur along the route from childhood to adulthood. This experience could be positive or negative, productive or nonproductive. In addition to describing this experience, the students needed to decide how many squares this experience would move them forward or backward on a scale of one to eight. Once the student(s) had created a square, it was glued onto the game board in an appropriate chronological spot. The range of experiences that students described on these squares was striking:

- "Your dog died. Move back two squares."
- "You smoked a cigarette for the first time. Move back one square."
- "You join a school sport. Move ahead four spaces."
- "You are late coming home and your mom asks why. You lie. Move back four squares."
- "You have your first sexual encounter. Move ahead five spaces."
- "You get straight 90s on your report card. Move ahead five."
- "You lose your cell phone. Move back eight."

The relative significance that the students assigned in scaling their experiences on these game squares reflected the widely varying perspectives and priorities of many of the students. For example, on one game board, "Your parents get divorced" moved the player back two squares, while "You've broken up with your girl/boy friend" moved the player back six squares.

The dilemma cards provided the students with an opportunity to describe a situation that they or other students had experienced in their lives—in or outside of school. They were asked to pose the dilemma, but not provide a solution. A sampling of these student-created dilemma cards provides an honest view of the day-to-day challenges faced by ninth graders. These student-written dilemmas reflect their overall focus on issues of friendship, relationship, loyalty, loss, and moral obligation.

You find out that your best friend's boy friend/girl friend is cheating on her/him. Do you tell your friend, knowing how hurt she/he will be OR do you keep it to yourself?

Your cousin dies and you miss her. You are sad and depressed. Nothing seems to matter anymore. What should you do?

You know that a friend who works with you at a store has been stealing from the register. Your boss blames you. If you tell your boss who is stealing the money, you will lose a friend. If you don't tell him, you may lose a job you really need. What do you do?

The local police have a warrant out for you because you stole some laptops from school and resold them. Do you turn yourself in and face time in a juvenile detention center or do you run away and try to hide at a relative's home in another state?

Once the game boards were completed and dilemma cards written, the students played the newly created game as a class in small, heterogeneous teams, rather than individually. When a team's playing piece landed on a dilemma square, the dilemma was read aloud by one of the team members and a decision as to how to respond was reached by consensus. Two significant patterns emerged across five classes as the board games created were played:

1. The number of squares that moved players back consistently outnumbered the squares that moved players ahead.
2. In three out of the five board games, the disproportionate number of negative or counterproductive squares, and where they were placed on the board, made the game impossible to win.

THE IMPACT OF FOCUSING ON SOCIAL-EMOTIONAL LEARNING THROUGH THE USE OF METAPHORS

To what degree did the activities and projects designed and implemented by the teaching team at Crossroads High School meet the academic, social, and emotional needs of incoming freshmen who have been identified as struggling learners? In answering this question, it is important to identify the impact of these educational initiatives on the students and on the faculty.

As a follow-up to playing the board game, students were asked to journal and then to share excerpts from their reflective writing with the instructors and with each other. The following sampling of responses describes some of the insights developed and connections made through this experiential process. They also illustrate the contradictions so commonly experienced and felt by many adolescents:

- "The board game we put together was my favorite activity because it helped me realize that in life you can take many steps forward, but you're gonna get pushed back some too."
- "Even though I didn't like the board game, it was helpful. It pointed things out to us, things that we didn't notice about ourselves and others."
- "The board game made me realize that we have more bad than good in our lives, and I agree."
- "Maybe if we weren't the ones who made the board game, it would have been possible to win."
- "The board game was helpful because it helped me experience things that happened before in my life and my friends' lives, and the things that could happen in the future."

Theorists who have studied interactive root metaphors describe their potential applications in teaching and learning as tools for discovery (Botha, 2009; Saban, 2006), communication (Botha), and as a medium for reflection and action planning (Black & Halliwell, 2000; Perry & Cooper, 2001: Saban, 2006). As this description of the Board Game Project illustrates, when students are engaged in exploring a metaphor that they find relevant and engaging—such as *journey*—powerful discovery, meaningful communication, and productive reflection and action planning can occur.

In addition to this important personal reflection and action planning, the faculty and consultant facilitating the metaphor-based activities observed several other significant student learning outcomes:

- Enhanced engagement in writing
- Development of problem solving skills
- Increased willingness and ability to work cooperatively
- Increased comfort with and engagement in self-study

While the primary focus of this innovative work was on supporting students' academic, social, and emotional growth and development, the teachers and administrators involved in the Crossroads High School Freshman Initiative Program recognized that the project produced several important outcomes for them and for the faculty as a whole, including:

- a broader understanding of the need to address social and emotional development when working with struggling students;
- increased willingness and ability to focus on social and emotional learning within subject area teaching;
- increased comfort with and ability to work collaboratively with colleagues across subject areas; and
- the creation and dissemination of instructional activities that focus on social and emotional learning.

CONCLUSION

As this chapter illustrates, productively and effectively engaging ninth-grade students who are in the midst of social, emotional, and academic transitions is a challenge to which all educators must respond. The use of root interactive metaphors in developing educational activities that are experiential, collaborative, and problem solving–oriented provides rich, evocative opportunities for student engagement and learning that support their success in school and in life.

REFERENCES

Black, A., & Halliwell, G. (2000). Accessing practical knowledge: How? Why? *Teaching and Teacher Education, 16*, 103–115.
Botha, E. (2009). Why metaphors matter in education. *South African Journal of Education, 29*, 431–444.
Campbell, J. (1949). *The hero with a thousand faces*. Princeton, NJ: Princeton University Press.
CASEL (Collaborative for Academic, Social, and Emotional Learning). (2011). *CASEL Brief: How evidence-based SEL programs work to produce greater student success in school and life*. Retrieved from http://casel.org/wp-content/uploads/2011/04/academicbrief.pdf
Durlak, J., Weissberg, R., & Pachan, M. (2010). A meta-analysis of after-school programs that seek to promote personal and social skills in children and adolescents. *American Journal of Community Psychology, 45*, 294–309.
Editorial Project in Education. (2010). Diplomas count 2010: Graduating by the number: Putting data to work for student success. *Education Week, 29*(34), 4–8.
Elbertson, N., Brackett, M., & Weissberg, R. (2010). School-based social and emotional learning (SEL) programming: Current perspectives. In A. Hargreaves, M. Fullan, A. Lieberman, & D. Hopkins (Eds.), *Second annual handbook of educational change* (pp. 1017–1035). New York, NY: Springer-Verlag.
Orfield, G. (2004). *Dropouts in America: Confronting the graduation rate crisis*. Cambridge, MA: Harvard University Press.
Payton, J., Weissberg, R., Durlak, J., Dymnicki, A., Taylor, R., Schellinger, K., et al. (2008). *The positive impact of social and emotional learning for kindergarten through eighth-grade students*. Chicago, IL: Collaborative for Academic, Social, and Emotional Learning (CASEL).
Perry, C., & Cooper, M. (2001). Metaphors are good mirrors: Reflecting on change for teacher educators. *Reflective Practice, 2*(1), 41–52.
Postman, N. (1996). *The end of education: Redefining the value of schools*. New York, NY: Knopf Doubleday.

Saban, A. (2006). Functions of metaphor in teaching and teacher education: A review essay. *Teaching Education, 17,* 299–315.

Tobin, K. (1990). Changing metaphors and beliefs: A master switch for teaching? *Theory Into Practice, 29,* 122–127.

U.S. Department of Education, National Center for Educational Statistics. (2010). *Digest for Educational Statistics 2009 (NCES 2010-013).* Washington, DC: U.S. Government Printing Office.

Zins, J., & Elias, M. (2006). Social and emotional learning. In G. Bear & K. Minke (Eds.), *Children's needs III: Development, prevention, and intervention* (pp. 1–13). Baltimore, MD: National Association of School Psychologists.

Chapter Eight

Making the Work Interesting: Classroom Management Through Ownership in Elementary Literature Circles

Ryan Flessner

Mr. Ellerton sat wondering what was happening in his classroom. He had been told over and over again that he needed a *discipline policy* in his fourth grade classroom. He had always rejected this idea for two reasons. First, he never believed that one system of management could appropriately address the strengths and needs of every child in a given classroom. Second, he always felt that truly engaging students in authentic work proactively created an environment co-managed by all members of a classroom community. Reading *Stuart Little* (White, 1945) for a children's literature class in his teacher education program, he had come across the following quote:

> "Do you think you can maintain discipline?" asked the Superintendent.
> "Of course I can," replied Stuart. "I'll make the work interesting and the discipline will take care of itself. Don't worry about me." (White, 1945, pp. 85–86)

"Yes," Mr. Ellerton thought to himself, "That makes sense."

In his first few years of teaching, he had heard veteran teachers say things like, "Don't smile before winter break. They (the students, he assumed) need to know you mean business." He had rejected this advice, choosing the *Stuart Little* approach instead. He was making decisions based on what he knew about each child; he offered his respect to the children assuming they would respect him in return. As a reflective teacher, he was anticipating problems and thinking through solutions prior to each lesson. To the chagrin of the veteran teachers, he often found himself smiling.

Thus far, his proactive system of management had seemed to be working. Yet, what had been happening for the past few days concerned Mr. Ellerton. While an outsider would say his students were well behaved, even teacher pleasers, he was frustrated. For the past several days, his students had been engaging in literature circle discussions.

As a class, he and his students had discussed the purposes and processes of literature circles. He had used his read-aloud time to model the types of thinking that he was doing as a reader. His fourth graders had shared their thoughts and ideas as they listened to the stories and seemed ready to engage in thoughtful conversations.

Unfortunately, what ensued was a series of what felt like *verbal worksheets*. Rather than capitalizing on the autonomy inherent in a literature circle discussion group, the students were reverting to practices in which they had engaged in previous classes throughout their educational experiences. They asked questions like, "What is the plot?" and "Who are the main characters?" To make things worse, the children were taking on traditional student/teacher roles. Rather than empowering themselves and their peers, they were exhibiting classic teacher-centered behaviors.

One child asked questions while the others raised their hands and waited patiently to be called on by the teacher. While students were respectful throughout the discussions, Mr. Ellerton knew the class was inching toward the slippery slope of boredom and, thus, disengagement. After watching these events unfold, Mr. Ellerton knew he had to make a change; he needed to *make the work interesting.*

THE EMERGENCE OF A PROBLEM: LACK OF STUDENT EMPOWERMENT

As a teacher, Mr. Ellerton wanted students to feel empowered and confident as readers and writers. He hoped to instill in his students a love for the written word. Because there are many examples of how literature circles promote student choice and control (Blum, Lipsett, & Yocom, 2002; Short, Kaufman, Kaser, Kahn, & Crawford, 1999), he decided to use this strategy as a key aspect of his reading instruction. Once he introduced the concept of literature circles, he assumed students would naturally engage in interesting, thoughtful dialogue. He was surprised that his students were unable to have authentic conversations when discussing a piece of literature.

Mr. Ellerton became concerned that students had misinterpreted the purposes of literature circles. Rather than experiencing literature circles as a form of self-empowerment, students used the time to reinforce traditional notions of reading comprehension. While the children were not "running around like crazy" as he had been warned they would, Mr. Ellerton had a different problem on his hands. Gradually, he realized his instruction was perpetuating many of the stereotypical classroom practices that he was trying to address.

To examine how he might rectify the problem he was having in his classroom, Mr. Ellerton turned to the readings that had inspired him to utilize literature circles in the first place (Casey, 2008; Clarke & Holwadel, 2007; Daniels, 2002; Zemelman, Daniels, & Hyde, 2005). Repeatedly, other teachers and educational researchers confirmed that literature circles were, in fact, a way to *make the work interesting*.

Yet, for some reason, Mr. Ellerton's initial attempts at implementation had failed to instill in his students the empowerment described in the literature. Therefore, he decided to rethink the ways that he could foster a community that empowered students and promoted thoughtful dialogue during literature circles.

RETHINKING LITERATURE CIRCLES

To begin, Mr. Ellerton had students write about their initial literature circle experiences in their journals. As he reviewed the journal entries, he realized that some students saw literature circles as a tool for understanding each other as learners. Others, however, seemed to emphasize more traditional aspects of reading instruction. As he reflected on the first round of literature circles, Mr. Ellerton repeatedly noted the difficulty children were having as they attempted to create natural discussions. Identifying this as the root of many of the patterns that seemed to be emerging, the teacher hatched a plan.

The following morning, Mr. Ellerton asked the children to take clipboards, paper, and a writing utensil with them during lunch and recess. Their task was to research how *real* conversations look and sound. Excitement mounted as students took on the task of investigative reporting. After their initial observations were captured, group journal entries were written and a classroom conversation ensued.

Through these creative activities, the children generated a checklist of what they hoped to accomplish during their literature circles. Though Mr. Ellerton was hesitant to standardize the literature circles even more, the students argued that a checklist would simply give them guidelines as they prepared for literature circles—it did not have to be used as a grading tool. In addition, the class (teacher *and* students) decided that the checklist could be used to assess what the groups were doing well and to identify areas where they needed further support. Topics on the checklist included the following:

- Getting Ready: Look for important ideas and examples of creative writing, be able to prove your point, ask divergent questions that have more than one answer.
- Group Work: Work together, debate—don't argue, focus on the group while doing your personal best.
- Discussions: Everyone speaks and participates, have a discussion—not a question/answer session, avoid interrupting.
- Speaking: Consider and add on to others' points, offer new ideas instead of repeating, stay on topic.

Once the checklist was finalized, the students were ready to begin analyzing their discussions. As a next step, students reviewed a videotape of a previously recorded literature circle. After viewing the videotape, students sat silently. When Mr. Ellerton asked how they thought the group had done, they erupted in laughter. This was not quite the response the teacher had expected. As he had feared, the students were using the checklist as a way to judge their peers.

Some students wrote about *power* in their journals. For instance, Jake stated, "[When I watch a videotape], I feel like I am the teacher and I get to grade kids on what they do." Others felt uneasy about the added responsibility of the checklist: "It is very hard to evaluate your friends because you don't want to say they're bad, but you don't want to lie when you are evaluating because it's to help them improve on literature circles," confided Callie.

After these comments from the students, Mr. Ellerton reminded the class that they had designed the checklist as a way to identify needs that would improve the literature circles. However, they had also discussed the importance of identifying areas of student strength. After this brief reminder, students became more willing to look for both needs and strengths in the literature circles.

Another problem encountered was that the students were providing no insight into how they had reached their judgments. They were simply placing a *yes* or *no* next to each item on the checklist. Early checklists contained little evidence to support evaluative claims made by the children. Students often had opinions about whether or not the groups were successful but could rarely support their claims.

After reviewing an early videotape, Mr. Ellerton asked his students to share their findings. Few raised their hands to offer comments. When asked why this was so, they commented that they were not sure they had given enough proof. Immediately, Mr. Ellerton changed his tactic. He collected the completed checklists and quickly glanced through the comments. As he came upon an evaluation that included justification, he read it to the class as a successful model. Therefore, students became more aware of what an exemplary response entailed. Mr. Ellerton hoped that this would make the children more willing to share their ideas.

Later, Mr. Ellerton identified this moment as a turning point in the classroom. Shortly after the conversation, students were running out of room to write on their sheets. Mr. Ellerton smiled as students asked for extra time to complete their checklists. He chuckled as some students took their papers to recess so they could squeeze in final comments. While personally gratifying for him as a teacher, Mr. Ellerton quickly realized that the true power came from the students themselves. The children were beginning to internalize the elements of a quality discussion—which they, *themselves*, had constructed—and were working to achieve this quality.

Beyond the students' increased abilities to identify important aspects of quality dialogue, literature circles improved in other ways as well. For instance, students regularly commented that interruptions were ruining the flow of the conversations. More conscious of this problem, the children began to listen to each other rather than interrupting their peers and showed enhanced lines of communication. When students listened, they began to consider each other's points, which led to friendly debates related to the readings. At one point, the following discussion took place:

Zoe: Do you relate to Charlie?

Tommy: I have this afterschool program that I go to. I've always just been the quiet kid. . . . I don't talk much.

Zoe: So you're shy, kind of?

Tommy: Yeah.

Zoe: Well, I don't think that Charlie was really shy. . . . No one really likes him because he's poor. So he probably feels like an outsider.

J.J. & Loren: Yeah.

Tommy: Yeah, I guess I see what you mean.

As this example shows, students were able to discuss their perceptions of the story, debate certain issues, and come to a consensus—or agree to disagree.

Other advantages were evident as students became more attuned to their peers and more empowered by the process. Many times, students were unable to debate because they all agreed with the comments of their classmate(s). In these situations, piggybacking became a useful tool. Students began to naturally experiment with this technique:

Starr: Ms. Trunchbull is so mean. I'd loathe having her as a headmistress. Why do you think she was so mean?

Callie: She's mean, and she just doesn't care. She seems to want to make you feel bad.

Jake: They said in the book that a good principal has to respect children and love them, but she has none of that. She pins them to the wall and tortures them like they're dolls or something.

Starr: She treats them like voodoo dolls.

Callie: Yeah, it reflects her life.

Students were moving away from a question/answer session, responding to one another, and creating effective dialogue through the use of the piggybacking strategy. As the semester progressed, Mr. Ellerton was pleased to realize that his work *with* the children was helping to *make the work interesting*.

CONCLUSION

Typical discussions of classroom management often revert to an examination of discipline policies. Teachers are often forced to take on the roles of authoritarians. Children are reduced to names on the board or marbles in a jar. Mr. Ellerton intuitively knew that there was more to managing a classroom. He knew that trust, respect, and empowerment were essential aspects of a strong learning community. He wanted students to understand that they could have power over their learning and that choice and control are not simply the responsibility of the teacher.

The story of Mr. Ellerton and his students highlights one example of a teacher examining his philosophies of educating children, rethinking his teaching, and empowering students to create mechanisms that would help them feel successful, accomplished, and engaged. Following Stuart Little's lead, Mr. Ellerton reimagined ways to proactively manage his classroom. Even when his attempts to support children seemed doomed, he stayed true to his beliefs.

As this narrative reveals, no longer does the phrase *classroom management* need to translate to *discipline plan*. Teachers everywhere can trade in sticker charts and penalty hall slips for lessons that are authentic, relevant, and engaging for students. In effect, teachers can *make the work interesting*.

Author's Note

All names are pseudonyms to protect the identity of those involved.

REFERENCES

Blum, H. T., Lipsett, L. R., & Yocom, D. J. (2002). Literature circles: A tool for self-determination in one middle school inclusive classroom. *Remedial and Special Education, 23,* 99–108.

Casey, H. K. (2008). Engaging the disengaged: Using literature clubs to motivate struggling adolescent readers and writers. *Journal of Adolescent & Adult Literacy, 52,* 284–294.

Clarke, L. W., & Holwadel, J. (2007). Help! What is wrong with these literature circles and how can we fix them? *The Reading Teacher, 61,* 20–29.

Daniels, H. (2002). *Literature circles: Voice and choice in book clubs and reading groups* (2nd ed.). Portland, ME: Stenhouse.

Short, K., Kaufman, G., Kaser, S., Kahn, L., & Crawford, M. (1999). "Teacher watching": Examining teacher talk in literature circles. *Language Arts, 76,* 377–385.

White, E. B. (1945). *Stuart Little.* New York, NY: Harper & Row.

Zemelman, S., Daniels, H., & Hyde, A. (2005). *Best practice: Today's standards for teaching and learning in America's schools.* Portsmouth, NH: Heinemann.

Chapter Nine

Students as Allies to Their Peers: Creating a Caring Majority

Karen Siris

The plight of the unaccepted child, the one who is chosen last, the one who is not included in social gatherings, the one who is called unkind names, or the one who is merely ignored, is often brought to the attention of school administrators by parents or the children themselves. It is incumbent upon school personnel, parents, and guardians to take these situations seriously, not only for the current and future social and emotional well-being of the child, but for his or her academic success as well.

Forty-nine states have passed antibullying and harassment laws making it imperative that schools have systems in place that prevent and intervene in situations that are causing pain for many schoolchildren (http://www.bullypolice.org/). It was with the tragic suicide of Tyler Clementi and the persistent and important lobbying of groups such as GLSEN (Gay, Lesbian & Straight Educational Network) that many pending bills finally become laws (Foderaro, 2012).

Research indicates that the bullying that takes place in the lives of the gay, lesbian, and transgender children surpasses the incidents of the heterosexual population (Kosciw & Diaz, 2006). Many states have required that there be a point person in each school to insure that all children are not only physically, but also emotionally safe throughout their days at school. In fact, many have now added protection from cyberbullying, bringing the school's responsibilities outside of the schoolhouse gates, if such harassment causes a substantial disruption to student learning.

THE PLAYERS

Teachers and administrators are being trained to understand the dynamics of bullying situations and to recognize their warning signs. Schools are also training parents to notice if their children may be targeted at school and, conversely, if their child is exhibiting bullying behaviors. They learn that children with bullying behaviors frequently come from homes where there is a lack of warmth, permissiveness, and/or aggression shown to them by a sibling or an adult.

Understanding the dynamics of a bullying situation and the players in the theater of harassment:—the bully (perpetrator), the victim (target), and the bystander—is necessary if teachers and administrators are going to foster positive change. In schools it is the bystander who hears and sees what is happening, yet often does not intervene. The data indicated that 85 percent of students are neither bully nor victim, but instead stand by as their classmates are either physically abused or emotionally alienated (Sagarese & Gianetti, 2003).

According to Sagarese and Gianetti (2003), "bystanders make or break bullying episodes" (p. 359). In their study of Canadian student bystanders, they found that 43 percent of respondents tried to help a victim. The remaining 57 percent stood by and watched, but did nothing. Of that number, 33 percent confessed that they should have attempted to help a victim but did not. Finally, 24 percent responded by saying that it was none of their business.

It is understood that bullying is an entrenched societal problem, one that causes thousands of children to suffer through childhood and adolescence. Yet it is the minority who are using their power to inflict the pain. The majority of students are bystanders, and now many think that these students hold the answer to ending this insidious problem in society. Establishing social norms in our schools that reward *upstanding* and frown upon *bullying* behaviors might hold the key (Phillips, Linney, & Pack, 2008).

CREATING A CARING CULTURE

Social learning theory postulates that peers, because they have undergone and survived relevant experiences, are more credible role models for others (Bandura, 1986). Interactions with peers who are successfully coping with their experiences result in positive behavior change. It makes sense, then, that the *caring majority* of students who speak up against bullying behaviors may solve an age-old problem.

If the silent majority of children—those that watch bullying behaviors take place—stand by helplessly, then they are implicitly allowing this to happen. If the majority of students are empowered, they will create a culture of positive behaviors that takes away the bully's audience and potentially strips the children with the bullying behaviors of their power. It is hypothesized that the influence of the silent majority could make the difference in so many young lives.

Bystanders have many reasons for standing by and not intervening. First and foremost, they fear becoming the next victim. They have watched what has happened to the targeted child and, above all else, do not want that happening to them. In addition, they often feel powerless to help the victim because they have not been taught the strategies to help. Sadly, they may have also lost confidence in the adults around them to help, so they stop reporting the incidents.

It is essential to establish a school culture that values the importance of a safe and nurturing environment. Without mutual respect among all constituents, asking students to stand up for each other will not be successful. With the high stakes testing and teacher evaluations that now hold so much importance for students as well as teachers, everyone should understand the value of an environment of caring and trust. Schools have to be welcoming places, where staff and students alike look forward to coming every day.

Teachers should be particularly aware of the child who is not easily assimilated with his or her peers, who may be lacking in social skills, and be sure to give him or her an extra special greeting each morning. Knowing that someone is happy to see us each day adds incentive to wanting to be in school to learn. The common element among schools reporting an increase in academic success, improved quality of relationships between teachers and students, and a decrease in problem behavior is a *systematic process* for promoting children's (and teachers') social and emotional growth (Greenberg et al., 2003). A teacher involved in an action research study focusing on eliminating bullying in classrooms wrote:

> Our feelings and our attitudes affect the whole room. Even if we don't realize what we are doing or how we're behaving, I think we send out signals subconsciously and the children pick them up. As soon as I focused on Farah's positive characteristics and spotlighted her in the classroom, everyone else looked at her that way, too. . . . She is now branching out to other children. If the girls she seeks out aren't very receptive, she joins another group. The other girls seem happy to have her. Things really changed for Farah. There is no question. (Siris, 2002, p. 103)

The teachers realized that by modeling positive and supportive interactions, by providing opportunities for students to work together in the classroom, and by developing class rules that value kindness and preclude exclusion, they support the development of positive peer relationships and minimize harassment.

EMPOWERING THE CARING MAJORITY

Schools that embrace a caring culture are turning to the bystanders to strip the power from the bully. Interested students apply for positions as caring majority ambassadors (Siris, 2003). Once accepted, they work alongside the social worker, psychologist, or principal to join in the efforts to end bullying behaviors.

The children wait anxiously, wondering if they will be accepted as caring ambassadors. They receive a confidential, congratulatory letter letting them know that they have been chosen for a special job in their school. The letter explains that with this position comes a big responsibility, one that requires their *best selves* to be displayed every day, because they are now role models for the rest of the students in our school.

The adult leader meets with the group to explain that the job carries big responsibilities and is not meant for just anyone. It involves missing some class time for training and many hours of recess time for small group work as they gather information for their presentations and skits. Any work missed in class has to be made up. It is rare that an accepted student ever turns down taking this responsibility. In fact, they are very proud to be selected. The letter asks for a parent and student signature indicating that the student accepts the position and its duties and that the parent approves as well.

CARING MAJORITY AMBASSADOR TRAINING

The children are welcomed on the day of training and thanked for volunteering to work to make their school a caring and welcoming place and for their commitment and willingness to give up some of their time to support the mission of creating a bully- and harassment-free school. They share their own stories and begin to form a bond with their fellow ambassadors.

The seriousness of bullying is discussed and poignant videos about what can happen are viewed. They already know quite a bit from their own experiences as well as what they have seen in the news about suicides and bullycides. It is important for the children to realize that bullying is rarely the sole reason for these suicides, and that there are other psychological and sociological components. It is stressed, however, that they would never want to hear that one child's unkindness to another ever had a part in the other child's desperate acts.

Information about the causes of bullying (psychological, familial, school), the characteristics of the bully, the victim, and the bystander, and the statistics about bullying in schools are introduced. A conversation about the importance of turning the children who stand by and watch (bystanders) into students who take a stand against bullying (upstanders) follows.

THE BYSTANDER

Even the youngest children you ask in elementary school understand the concept of the bystander. They do because they have all been in the situation of passively watching bullying behaviors take place. When asked why they don't speak up, invariably the same answers are heard:"I am afraid the bully will make me the next person he teases," or "I am afraid he will turn all my friends against me," or "I don't know what to say to the bully."

The older children also say, "I have reported it to adults before, but nothing ever happens. Even when the bully gets a consequence, he does it again, and again, and again." The children reveal that they often feel powerless and that they do not have the words or tools to stand up to the bully.

The ambassadors come to understand that the bystanders provide the audience a bully craves and the silent acceptance that allows bullies to continue their hurtful behavior. They realize that passively accepting bullying by watching and doing nothing is not acceptable. They learn that encouraging the bullying by laughing or cheering actually makes them complicit in the bullying situation, without having been the one who actually initiated it. Through discussion, the ambassadors agree that the key to stopping bullying would be to turn the *silent majority of bystanders* into a *caring majority of upstanders*.

Through discussion and role-playing, the new ambassadors realize that being able to speak up for their friends takes courage. Through "The Youth Voice Research Project," Davis and Nixon (2010) surveyed 13,000 targeted students to find out what they considered to be the most effective interventions by peers. The results indicated improvement when their peers did the following:

- spent time with those bullied;
- talked to them;
- helped them get away; and
- called them after the incident to see how they were doing.

The least effective interventions included blaming the target, ignoring the situation, and confronting the bully.

THE ALLIES

The term *allies* is used to define the children who befriend the targeted child, and it suggests that at least two or three allies work together when confronting a bullying situation. It stands to reason that if bullying behaviors involve an imbalance of power, with the bully wielding this power, it will take more than one child to ask him or her to stop. If a group of children come to the aid of a target, it begins to strip the bullies of their powers, thereby isolating them with no audience for their unkindness.

THE AMBASSADORS' WORK

Once given the background knowledge about bullying and strategies to empower the bystanders, the ambassadors get to work. They divide into small teams and through consensus choose a lower grade level as their audience. They take the information they have learned and create their own PowerPoint presentations and skits to inform their younger classmates how to become *upstanders* and members of the caring majority in their school. They take their work very seriously and come during their recess time to develop their plan.

An adult mentor helps them edit and revise their presentations and, when they are ready, schedules a grade level presentation for each of the groups. It is inspirational to watch how students take ownership of the work they are doing and how they feel responsible for imparting what they have learned to their younger classmates.

Each new group of ambassadors shares its commitment and dedication to teaching all the children in the school how to become *upstanders.* The younger students listen attentively to the ambassadors as they stand in front of them and teach them about kindness, caring, and inclusion and as they give them the tools to become helpful allies to their peers.

The ambassadors continue the work with their young students throughout the year. They visit their classrooms, share lunch tables, and spend time during recess. They are there as role models and friends to their younger classmates. They listen to their problems and help them find solutions as they develop powerful and lifelong bonds.

CONCLUSION

A school community that values the importance of kindness and inclusion and that teaches its students strategies for standing up for others understands the importance of creating a positive school climate. Empowering students to become mentors to their peers as caring majority ambassadors can enhance a positive school culture.

The adults in the community, including all staff members as well as parents, must speak the same language as the students and exhibit the same behaviors in their daily lives. Once this is achieved, perhaps we will make progress in changing the dynamics of bullying, an age-old problem. Educators must continue to realize that, to reach high academic goals, they must not forget the social and emotional needs of the students. The time spent creating positive relationships among all members of the school community is most valuable and essential.

REFERENCES

Bandura, A. (1986). *Social foundations of thought and action.* Englewood Cliffs, NJ: Prentice-Hall.

Davis, S., & Nixon, C. (2010). *The Youth Voice Research Project.* Retrieved from http://www.youthvoiceproject.com/YVPMarch2010.pdf

Foderaro, L.W. (2010, September 29). Private moment made public, then a fatal jump. *New York Times.* Retrieved from http://www.nytimes.com/2010/09/30/nyregion/30suicide.html?pagewanted=all&_r=0

Greenberg, M. T., Weissberg, R. P., O'Brien, M. U., Zins, J. E., Fredericks, L., Resnik, H., et al., (2003). Enhancing school-based prevention and youth development through coordinated social, emotional, and academic learning. *American Psychologist, 58,* 466–474.

Kosciw, J. G., & Diaz, E. M. (2006). *The 2005 National School Climate Survey: The experiences of lesbian, gay, bisexual, and transgender youth in our nation's schools.* New York, NY: Gay, Lesbian and Straight Education Network. Retrieved from http://www.glsen.org/binary-data/GLSEN_ATTACHMENTS/file/585-1.pdf

Phillips R., Linney J., & Pack, C. (2008). *Safe school ambassadors: Harnessing student power to stop bullying and violence.* Indianapolis, IN: Jossey-Bass.

Sagarese, M., & Giannetti, C. (2003). *The bystander: A bully's often-unrecognized accomplice.* Retrieved from http://www.papta.org/Page/359

Salzer, M., & Shear, S. L. (2002). Identifying consumer-provider benefits in evaluations of consumer-delivered services. *Psychiatric Rehabilitation Journal, 25,* 281–288.

Siris, K. (2002). *Using action research to alleviate bullying and victimization in the classroom.* Unpublished doctoral dissertation, Hofstra University, Hempstead, NY.

Siris, K. (2003, October). Creating a caring community: One school's plan to ban bullying. *ASCD Classroom Leadership, 7*(2). Retrieved from http://www.ascd.org/publications/classroom-leadership/oct2003/Creating-a-Caring-Community.aspx

Chapter Ten

Cracking the Behavior Code: Effective Interventions for Students with Anxiety

Jessica Minahan and Nancy Rappaport

Identifying the triggers for inappropriate behaviors and teaching children more desirable responses can be part of intervention plans in any classroom.

When anxiety is an underlying cause of a student's behavior, traditional behavioral supports can be not just unhelpful, but can even exacerbate a student's behavior, leading to acting out, self-harm, suspensions, and perhaps even school avoidance. To succeed in school, students with anxiety need a prescribed behavioral intervention plan that addresses their anxiety, explicitly, teaches the underdeveloped skills contributing to it, and helps students learn more appropriate alternative responses. It should also include accommodations teachers can use while students learn these skills.

Traditional behavioral plans for children with anxiety often neglect to outline the skills they must learn to manage their anxiety and strengthen the contributing underdeveloped skills. Often school personnel will identify a desirable target behavior and try to reinforce it through rewards, such as stickers or praise. Usually this approach does not work. When educators do not recognize that anxiety prompts some behaviors—for example, melt-downs or withdrawal—their responses may unintentionally heighten a student's inappropriate behavior.

Consider Stephanie, a fourth grader with generalized anxiety disorder, who struggles with writing. When given a writing assignment, she whines, asks to go to the nurse, or cries. When a preferred activity ends—art or a computer game—she may scream, "You're always picking on me! I hate school!" She might have outbursts while doing her favorite activity. Her teacher describes her behavior as sometimes "coming out of the blue."

THE EFFECT OF ANXIETY

A student with high anxiety can fall behind academically because he or she is anxious and distracted, resulting in impaired verbal working memory skills (Hopko, Crittendon, Grant, & Wilson, 2005). One study showed that first graders who were the most anxious in the fall were much more likely to have lower math and reading achievement in the spring (Ialongo & Edelsohn, 1994).

Often anxious children must exert more effort to perform well because they are trying to manage their anxiety while executing a task (Owens, Stevenson, Norgate, & Hadwin, 2008). If untreated, anxiety can persist for years (Mychailyszyn, Mendez, & Kendall, 2010), but proper interventions can decrease anxiety and improve learning (Ozsivadjian, Knott, & Magiati, 2012).

Behavioral Attributes of Students with Anxiety

Some students with anxiety show consistent and recognizable signs, such as flushed cheeks and tense muscles. Often, however, we do not know a student is feeling anxious until we see behavioral signs. These students can be hard to identify, but teachers can learn to recognize and understand the behavioral signs.

The child's behavior can mimic other students with low frustration tolerance or chronically oppositional profiles (Barrett & Heubeck, 2000; Garland & Garland, 2001). They may yell, kick, cry, leave the classroom, or be frustrated. What sets them apart is the underlying cause of their oppositional behavior. Fortunately, there are some standard behavioral symptoms that help us recognize underlying anxiety. (See Table 10.1.)

Inconsistent Patterns of Behavior

Anxiety is a hidden disability. For teachers, the inconsistent and erratic nature of anxiety-related behavior can be baffling. Stephanie breaks her pencil on Monday and calmly asks the teacher for another. On Tuesday, the same child breaks her pencil and screams, cries, and runs out of the room—an outburst having little to do with the broken pencil. Unbeknownst to the teacher, Stephanie's anxiety level was extremely high that day, so it looked as if her behavior came *out of nowhere.*

Let us use the analogy of a shaken soda can. Unless you see it happen, you cannot know it had been shaken just by looking at it. You find out when you open the can and it explodes. The same thing is true with students who

Classic attributes	Less obvious attributes
• Is easily frustrated • Complains of physical pains, such as stomach aches and headaches; has trouble breathing • Exhibits fear • Seems on the lookout for danger • Upset easily by mistakes (perfectionism) • Cries • Startles easily • Blushes, trembles • Expresses worry frequently	• Has difficulty completing work • Acts irritable • Acts angry • Does not follow school rules • Has inconsistent patterns in antecedents • Exhibits ritualistic or repetitive behavior • Is inflexible • Acts out spontaneously; seems over-reactive

Table 10.1 *Behavioral Attributes of Anxiety in Schools*

have anxiety-related behavior—often they look fine and then inexplicably explode.

In addition to behavior fluctuations, performance can also vary due to anxiety's effects on working memory, attention, and other abilities. Unfortunately, when teachers observe a student writing two beautiful paragraphs one day, then struggling to write a single sentence the next, they may come to the erroneous conclusion the student is lazy or unmotivated.

Avoidant Behavior

Understanding the function of the behavior is key. A student's anxiety-related behavior is often motivated by escape or avoidance. Most teachers recognize that when a student like Stephanie asks to go to the nurse before a writing assignment, this may be avoidant behavior. Sometimes it is less obvious. The student may start swearing or put her head down on the desk during a math test. If the teacher responds with a time-out or sends her to the office, the teacher may accidentally reinforce the avoidant behavior because the student has delayed the assignment.

WHY TRADITIONAL BEHAVIOR PLANS DO NOT WORK

Traditional behavior plans, like sticker charts, point systems, and level systems, are based on rewards and consequences. For instance, "If you don't interrupt in math class, you'll earn five points toward your computer time." Conversely, "If you interrupt in math class, you'll lose two minutes of recess." Typically, the criteria for behavior are set and inflexible, based on the student's abilities when she is calm and not taking into account her fluctuating level of anxiety or variable ability to behave and perform (Minahan & Rappaport, 2012).

In math class, Stephanie could achieve the expectation of being quiet and attentive. But when her reading class has to pick partners, she may become anxious and start to act out. She is not able to meet the behavioral criteria due to trouble with self-regulation, impulse control, and flexible thinking when she is anxious. Students with anxiety may show minimal or no behavioral improvement with a traditional behavioral plan. This can lead to resentment as they fail to meet expectations and continue to receive negative feedback on their behavior.

BEHAVIOR AS A RESULT OF UNDERDEVELOPED SKILLS

Students with anxiety would behave if they were able. When they cannot, it is often because the following skills may be underdeveloped:

- Self-regulation—The ability to self-calm and manage frustration
- Thought stopping/thought interruption—The ability to short-circuit the cycle of negative thinking by refocusing attention on a replacement thought
- Recognition of thinking traps—The ability to recognize and manage repetitive or negative thought patterns
- Social skills—The ability to participate in conversations and accept another person's perspective
- Executive functioning—The ability to think before acting, following sequential steps to complete tasks efficiently
- Flexible thinking—The ability to be more flexible when anxious, so they will not become upset when situations do not go their way

These skills must be explicitly taught if the student is to change behavior over the long term. Sadly, many behavior plans/programs never address these skills.

PREVENTION AS INNOVATION

When reflecting on a behavior incident, teachers should learn how to identify what happened just before the inappropriate behavior (antecedents) and how peers and the teacher responded (consequences). This is more important than focusing on the specific details of the incident.

Although students with anxiety can have inconsistent behavior, these antecedents routinely emerge as problematic:

- Unstructured times, such as lunch and recess
- Transitions
- Writing demands
- Social demands

• Novel events/unexpected change

Ninety percent of every behavior plan should be dedicated to antecedent management (Minahan & Rappaport, 2012). Accommodations that reduce anxiety-provoking situations/activities are crucial to helping a student reduce or eliminate inappropriate behavior. A student will continue to require accommodations until he or she develops the coping skills to manage anxiety and can succeed without them.

Catch It Early

The best way to bypass a student's surprising emotional outburst is to intervene early. A safe, observable definition of anxiety that teachers can use is *any sudden change in behavior* on the part of the student (Crisis Prevention Institute, 2008). Obviously, there can be many reasons other than anxiety for a sudden change in behavior—for example, pinching a finger or needing to go the bathroom. However, when a student has chronic emotional outbursts, it is a good rule of thumb that anxiety might be the culprit.

When a teacher observes a behavior change—for instance when a student who was calmly working starts to argue—the teacher has the opportunity for a check-in. ("How's it going?" "Need a drink of water?" "Anything bothering you?") This can stop the anxiety from magnifying and overwhelming the student and, most important, prevent the student from losing time on learning because of off-task behavior.

Environmental Accommodations

Teachers should have anxiety management in place throughout the day to avoid overwhelming a student, possibly provoking a behavioral incident. Implementing anxiety-reducing breaks consistently is an accommodation that helps settle students and keep them calm. Students should not have to earn breaks, nor should breaks be withheld because of behavior. A good starting point is two 10-minute breaks a day. This allows teachers to learn more about what helps individual students.

Make sure the break does not include anxiety-producing stimuli. For example, if Stephanie finds social interaction stressful, taking a friend on her break is not calming. If she has to work hard to process language, her break should be conversation free. Ideally, the break should involve movement. If there is concern that the student overuses breaks as an escape, the teacher can assign a maximum number of *break cards* and teach the student how to budget them.

Unstructured times, such as lunch and recess, may provoke anxiety. They often require social skills (e.g. deciding where to sit or whom to play with), executive functioning skills (e.g. organizing getting lunch), and self-regulation skills (e.g. staying calm in a chaotic environment). Providing alternative lunch and/or recess settings can help a student to succeed and be more regulated during the afternoon.

Teachers can facilitate a successful alternative-lunch social interaction between the student and two peers in a small, quiet space, and/or an alternative recess with a few peers in a separate location. This may allow the student to be more settled throughout the remainder of the day (Minahan & Rappaport, 2012).

Transitions throughout the day can also be difficult. Students require a lot of flexibility to stop an activity and executive functioning skills to organize and plan for the next activity. Providing transition supports during these times can help (for more details, see Minahan & Rappaport, 2012).

Academic Accommodations

Students with anxiety also need academic accommodations. The teacher can begin by presenting only a few activities at a time and breaking down directions into small, achievable steps. Teachers can preview all of the student's least favorite activities in the morning by explaining the assignment and actually showing the work. For example, the teacher can show Stephanie the math worksheet and start the first problem with her. Later that day, when the teacher hands out the math sheet, Stephanie will be less likely to become anxious and more able to initiate the task.

Students with anxiety tend to be all-or-nothing thinkers and inaccurate about their writing. We prefer to have a student say, "I'm not a great speller, but I have a strategy," rather than, "I hate writing" or "I'm a horrible writer." One method is for students to keep a chart of those aspects of writing assignments they find challenging, along with a list of available coping strategies they can use when stuck. (For example, when a student cannot expand on an idea, the chart tells him to search images on the computer.) After a while, the chart may help the student realize he or she has less need of the coping strategies than previously thought.

Self-regulation

Self-regulation is the ability to have control over one's emotions and behavior. Cognitive Behavioral Therapy and self-monitoring techniques are integral parts of teaching self-regulation, which benefits students with anxiety. Many students are unable to identify their emotions. They do not understand that emotions start small and grow larger—from calm to explosive in a split second. An *emotional thermometer* is an effective tool for teachers to use to label the child's emotions/arousal state throughout the day.

Body checks are another way to educate students about their emotions and arousal states (Minahan & Rappaport, 2012). Narrating the behavior clues for students, while indicating their feelings, can help them understand what an emotion *feels* and *looks* like. The teacher may say: "I notice your face is scrunched, your shoulders are up near your ears, and your fist is clenched. You're frustrated right now." Or "Your voice is very high-pitched and loud, you're talking fast, and you're moving around in your chair. You seem anxious." In time, students will learn to identify the emotion they are feeling, which is the first step to regulating it.

Students can then learn to catch themselves at the frustration point and practice a coping strategy to self-regulate before becoming explosive or shutting down. Adding corresponding self-regulation strategies on the emotional thermometer (see Figure 10.1) is helpful for cueing the student: "I think you're getting frustrated. What strategy are you going to use?"

Many of our students do not know how to self-calm, so explicit instruction and practice in self-calming skills is important. The student can benefit from practicing as often as twice a day, especially in the place where he may be taken when upset (guidance office, quiet corner of the classroom). This can foster automaticity of the skills when they are in that space during an actual behavior incident.

Calming boxes contain small items the student can keep in a box for use in times of stress, such as putty, a good-luck charm, or noise-reducing headphones (Minahan & Rappaport, 2012). As with other behavior modifications, the student needs to learn when and where to use the items to self-regulate behavior. Stephanie learned to carry a lucky penny that helped her remain calm during transitions in the building and in loud assemblies.

Reinforcement

Without using punishment and rewards for appropriate behavior, many teachers may be unclear on how to reinforce a student with anxiety. Taking time to build relationships with students helps create a supportive and safe classroom environment. Non-contingent reinforcement (NCR) is very powerful (Cooper, Heron, & Heward, 2007). It is a teacher's *random act of kindness*, like giving Stephanie a cool pencil, and saying "just because I like you." This shows she is not only appreciated when she is behaving, but also that the teacher really likes her as a person.

Assigning positive reinforcement—like points or tokens for practicing social or self-regulation skills, as well as using a strategy in difficult moments—promotes learning and reinforces the student's practice and application of their underdeveloped skills. Rather than having Stephanie earn points for *good* behavior (as is typically done with traditional plans, e.g., "five

Feeling	Strategies
Angry 	Take a break; deep breaths
Frustrated 	Get a drink; use my calming box
Excited 	Take deep breaths
Anxious 	Use my calming box
Sad 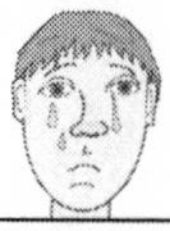	Use my words; use my calming box
Content 	Use my words
Happy 	Use my words; smile or laugh.

Figure 10.2.   Emotional Thermometer

points for doing your work"), she earns points for practicing deep breathing, using a calming box, and so on.

Stephanie learned to take deep breaths, to identify when she was anxious in some situations, and to use her writing strategies checklist and calming box. Understanding Stephanie's behavior, her teacher helped her learn to take breaks and use prescribed accommodations. She also gave her explicit instruction in executive functioning, flexible thinking, and taking perspective. Stephanie learned to use self-regulation strategies by earning bonus points whenever she used a strategy or practiced self-calming during the day.

CONCLUSION

Traditional behavior plans often do not meet the needs of students with anxiety and may even exacerbate inappropriate behavior. Understanding the role that anxiety plays in a student's behavior is crucial, as is analyzing how the environment and the school's responses may unintentionally reinforce negative behavior.

An effective behavior plan needs to avoid reward/punishment-based consequences and, instead, focus on teaching the student to cope and to use alternative responses while strengthening their underdeveloped skills. Incorporating preventative strategies and self-monitoring systems in school-based settings must be part of an overall anxiety-management approach to behavior.

REFERENCES

Barrett, S., & Heubeck, B. G. (2000). Relationships between school hassles and uplifts and anxiety and conduct problems in grades 3 and 4. *Journal of Applied Developmental Psychology, 21*, 537–554.

Cooper, J. O., Heron, T. E., & Heward, W. L. (2007). *Applied behavior analysis*. Upper Saddle River, NJ: Pearson/Merrill Prentice Hall.

Crisis Prevention Institute. (2008). *Instructor manual for the Nonviolent Crisis Intervention® training program*. Milwaukee, WI: Crisis Prevention Institute.

Garland, E. J., & Garland, O. M. (2001). Correlation between anxiety and oppositionality in a children's mood and anxiety disorder clinic. *Canadian Journal of Psychiatry, 46*, 953–958.

Hopko, D. R., Crittendon, J. A., Grant, E., & Wilson, S. A. (2005). The impact of anxiety on performance IQ. *Anxiety, Stress & Coping, 18*(1), 17–35.

Ialongo, N., & Edelsohn, G. (1994). The significance of self-reported anxious symptoms in 1st-grade children. *Journal of Abnormal Child Psychology, 22*, 441–456.

Minahan, J., & Rappaport, N. (2012). *The behavior code: A practical guide to understanding and teaching the most challenging students*. Cambridge, MA: Harvard Education Press.

Mychailyszyn, M. P., Mendez, J. L., & Kendall, P. C. (2010). School functioning in youth with and without anxiety disorders: Comparisons by diagnosis and comorbidity. *School Psychology Review, 39*(1), 106–121.

Owens, M., Stevenson, J., Norgate, R., & Hadwin, J. A. (2008). Processing efficiency theory in children: Working memory as a mediator between trait anxiety and academic performance. *Anxiety, Stress & Coping, 21*, 417–430.

Ozsivadjian, A., Knott, F., & Magiati, I. (2012). Parent and child perspectives on the nature of anxiety in children and young people with autism spectrum disorders: A focus group study. *Autism: The International Journal of Research & Practice, 16*(2), 107–121.

Chapter Eleven

Warm Demander Pedagogy: Managing Behavior Through the 3 R's of Insistence

Barbara Berté, Micheline Malow, and Diane W. Gómez

Rowan, a 16-year-old African American young man with a history of violent episodes and oppositional behavior in the classroom, started ninth grade like the years before, exchanging verbal abuse with classmates that sometimes resulted in physical altercations. Ms. Bee knew that there had to be more to Rowan but struggled with how to bring it out of him; realizing that earning Rowan's respect, rather than demanding it, would lead to a much more productive dynamic. So she began to actively cultivate their relationship.

"How are things going today Rowan?" "Nice to see you." "What don't you understand?" "Can I help you with that?" Common pleasantries to some, not so common to others. From the beginning of the school year, Ms. Bee actively cultivated a relationship based on respect and trust with this young man despite his difficult behaviors. Then seemingly out of nowhere, one day Rowan reached out to Ms. Bee for advice with a personal issue he was struggling with; a noticeable departure from his typically hardened exterior.

Ms. Bee listened, truly listened and through this Rowan heard loud and clear—Ms. Bee cared about him as a person, as well as about his success in school. When this episode was repeated and Rowan approached her for a second time, Ms. Bee recognized what a significant step she had made toward the successful cultivation of a relationship with him.

There are many students who have never felt a connection to a school or a teacher, students who act out in inappropriate and unacceptable ways as a means of task avoidance, and students who place little value on their academics because they seem to place little value on themselves and their futures. In short, students like Rowan who have walled themselves inside thick, hardened exteriors as a way to protect their fragility.

How can educators help these students who are so desperately in need of someone to take action—to change the course of their destiny? As a reflective practitioner, Ms. Bee struggled with this very question. Wanting nothing more than her students' success, Ms. Bee reached out to her colleagues for advice that could guide her practice.

Teachers make many attempts to reach disenfranchised students, including establishing high expectations for students' learning, recognizing cultural knowledge, incorporating community issues into the classroom, viewing knowledge critically, and valuing students; however, often these attempts are not enough (Hyland, 2009). The link between the negative perceptions that students hold of teachers and subsequent student performance suggests that in order to be highly effective with urban students, teachers may need to look beyond the curriculum and traditional classroom management pedagogy.

WARM DEMANDER PEDAGOGY

Through a conversation with a colleague and her own research, Ms. Bee learned about a pedagogy that aligned with her philosophy of education. This pedagogy fosters personal relationships with students, which in turn allows for the nonnegotiable demand of academic effort and success from those students by using the calm voice of insistence (Bondy, Ross, Gallingame, & Hambacher, 2007). What Ms. Bee found was *warm demander pedagogy*, and it was about to change her teaching practice forever.

Warm demander pedagogy focuses on the concepts of building relationships and communities within the classroom dynamic. The teachers who utilize this practice express concerns about their students' lives and interests and incorporate discussions about race into their curriculum.

What makes warm demander pedagogy unique is its seemingly counterintuitive practices: establishing both a caring personal relationship with students while countering this relationship with tireless and unbendable high academic and behavioral expectations. In actuality, it is the warm personal relationship that allows for the relentless demands of high academic achievement (Bondy et al., 2007).

Teachers utilizing this approach exhibit an authoritative tone when engaging their students. This insistent tone is labeled as "not ask but tell" with voices characterized as "not harsh but steeped in affinity" (Ullucci, 2009, p.

26). Ross, Bondy, Gallingame, and Hambacher (2008) advocated that "one key strategy in creating a positive psychological environment is the teacher's capacity to 'insist' that the students meet established academic and behavioral standards" (p. 142).

Insistence is characterized by repeated and respectful requests and the calm delivery of consequences. It is communicated through the following practices: (a) the explicit and clear-cut communication of expectations, (b) a pattern of repeat, remind, and reinforce in which those clear-cut expectations are reintroduced to students daily, and (c) communication with students delivered in a tone of voice that is calm and respectful, yet firm and direct (Bondy et al., 2007).

Ms. Bee could hardly contain her enthusiasm with the discovery of this practice. Could warm demander pedagogy be the answer for her classroom?

WARM DEMANDER PEDAGOGY IN ACTION

Ms. Bee is the general education teacher in a ninth grade Global History Collaborative Team Teaching (CTT) class. Her school represents a typical inner-city public high. The majority of the student population is students of color, receiving Title 1 funding, and one quarter of the class is serviced with an Individualized Education Plan (IEP).

In this academic setting, which was very different from her own high school experience, Ms. Bee was confronted with students who exhibited both negative and impulsive behaviors in the classroom. She chose to implement warm demander pedagogical practices with two Hispanic and two African American students: Enrique, Geraldo, Jovan, and Rowan.

Ms. Bee developed a chart to track her students' behaviors of (a) calling out, (b) using vulgarity or profanity, (c) bullying, (d) getting out of their seat without permission, and (e) using threats of violence and her implementation of the 3 R's: (a) repeat, (b) remind, and (c) reinforce (See Table 11.1).

The 3 R's

Classes are rife with instances of students ignoring a teacher's first behavioral request. Enacting warm demander pedagogy, teachers respond firmly and respectfully to students when negative behavior is displayed, utilizing the practice of insistence. The art of insistence uses the 3 R's of repeat, remind, and reinforce, in a nonpunitive way. Consistency of implementation reinforces that the teacher means what he or she says.

For implementation, the first response is to repeat the request, in a calm, yet authoritative tone. The repetition of the demand is delivered matter-of-factly using the same tone as the initial request. If several repetitions prove ineffective, the teacher clearly reminds the student of the expectation. Re-

	Enrique	Geraldo	Jovan	Rowan
Teacher Remediation Remind				
Teacher Remediation Repeat				
Teacher Remediation Reinforce				
Student Behavior Calling out				
Student Behavior Profanity/Vulgarity				
Student Behavior Bullying				
Student Behavior Getting out of seat				
Student Behavior Violence				

Table 11.1

Behavior Chart

minders can be verbal or nonverbal, with the goal that students recognize their behavior is out of compliance. Nonverbal reminders may include the teacher modeling the expected behavior and/or moving closer to a student to encourage engagement in the required task (i.e., proximity control).

The final step is reinforcement, used to increase student efforts of engaging in appropriate behavior. It can consist of the typical verbal praises or nonverbal reinforcement. Furthermore, consequences of noncompliance also serve to reinforce expectations. Whenever a student continues with noncompliant behavior, warm demander pedagogy seeks to view these repeated difficulties as a puzzle to be solved and the teacher returns to the beginning with relationship building.

How did the application of the 3 R's look in Ms. Bee's class? Let's examine the results, with the four students selected for this intervention.

Rowan

The beginning scenario described how Rowan exhibited both violent tendencies and oppositional behavior. Following warm demander pedagogy, Ms. Bee actively sought to establish foundations of trust and caring with Rowan.

The effectiveness of warm demander pedagogy was tested during an Egyptian History Jeopardy game activity. Rowan and another student engaged in a verbal argument that quickly escalated in both volume and severity. Throughout the incident, Ms. Bee used physical proximity and a low, nonconfrontational, yet insistent tone. She continued to calmly repeat, remind, and reinforce to Rowan that he needed to stop arguing with the other student.

While Rowan did initially lose his temper, he eventually calmed down without the incident escalating into violence. Rowan seemed to recognize, even in the tense moment, that Ms. Bee truly cared about his safety and well-being. It is this unequivocal communication of teacher caring that allows for disenfranchised students like Rowan to transform their lives.

The *authoritative* rather than *authoritarian* tone proved to be successful in reaching Rowan and not alienating him within that emotionally heightened moment. The incident was successfully diffused without violence or further ramifications. As a result of warm demander practices, Rowan was able to self-regulate in a way that he had not been able to even contemplate in previous years.

Geraldo

Geraldo's behavior typically manifested itself in impulsive calling out throughout class as well as the occasional bullying of several targeted students. He, along with Enrique and Jovan, would make derogatory comments directed at specific students in the class. His behavior was so severe that he received a significant amount of time of in-school suspension. He exhibited impulsive behavior that went beyond simple task avoidance and frequently led him into trouble. Ms. Bee worked diligently in her attempts to cultivate a relationship with Geraldo in order to open the door to successfully remediating his behavior. Initially, these efforts did not meet with much success.

A breakthrough occurred when Ms. Bee used Geraldo's interest in video games to foster the beginning of a teacher-student relationship based on respect. Ms. Bee casually remarked that she knew that Geraldo was very knowledgeable about video games. She asked if Geraldo could give her advice about earphones to buy her son for the video game he played. The utilization of a personal approach, the recognition of his interests, and the opening up of the teacher about her personal life provided the first steps in developing a warm demander relationship. This breakthrough with Geraldo and the corresponding establishment of trust and respect had an enormous impact on Geraldo's behavior, revealing the importance of building relationships.

Prior to the implementation of warm demander strategies in the classroom, Geraldo would have remained oppositional when faced with any type of remediation, regardless of tone. Through the implementation of warm demander strategies, Geraldo was receptive, thereby allowing dialogue to occur. He was then able to communicate his own feelings about his behavior and he recognized that on many occasions he exhibited inappropriate behavior that had a disruptive impact on the rest of the class.

It was the open and respectful dialogue facilitated by warm demander pedagogy that continued Geraldo's self-regulation of behavior. Additionally, while he occasionally would impulsively call out, the 3 R's proved to be a very effective means to encourage Geraldo to exhibit appropriate behavior and minimize disruptive ones. The firm communication and reminder of the clear cut classroom expectations utilized by Ms. Bee were based upon the successful incorporation of the structure of insistence (Bondy et al., 2007).

Enrique

Enrique's diagnosis of Attention Deficit Hyperactivity Disorder was so extreme that he was simply unable to remain seated for any extended period of time. He could not attend to classroom activities and oftentimes blurted out inappropriate, vulgar, and at times racist and homophobic comments aimed at other students.

Enrique seemed incapable of self-regulation. These negative behaviors were juxtaposed with promising academic potential. When Enrique was capable of attending, his academic skills were on target. As with Geraldo, Enrique tended to react in an oppositional manner when approached about his behavior. Past experience showed that if Enrique was having a bad day, it would manifest itself in multiple episodes of his leaving his seat and calling out in class.

Enrique and Geraldo, who were good friends, would often feed off each other's negative energy, and the unfortunate effects would be disastrous for the rest of the class. However, this close friendship actually benefitted Ms. Bee in the cultivation of respectful teacher-student relationships with both students. As Geraldo began to embrace the teacher-student dynamic that was being developed, so eventually did Enrique. It was the positive role model that his friend became that encouraged Enrique to stop being so oppositional.

Enrique started reaching out to Ms. Bee between classes, at lunch, and even to avoid going to other classes. Ms. Bee would use the time spent walking Enrique back to his assigned class to continue a respectful and open dialogue. Enrique's mother had passed away when Enrique was five years old, and on several occasions Enrique referred to Ms. Bee as "mom." This other-*mother role* provided the opening for Ms. Bee to successfully incorporate the practices of insistence with Enrique and to remind him of classroom expectations.

Jovan

Jovan was perhaps the most oppositional student in Ms. Bee's class. He repeatedly bullied other students by physically pushing them and calling out insults. Part of his typical behavior was to scream out derogatory comments directed at his victims. When cited for his negative behaviors, Jovan consistently appeared unremorseful and resistant.

Regardless, Ms. Bee consistently applied the 3 R's of insistence in an attempt to encourage Jovan to change his behavior. She was always careful to use a nonthreatening, yet assertive tone with him. Ms. Bee believed that Jovan would view *asking* rather than *telling* as weakness and, therefore, would diminish the impact on his behaviors. She recognized that a stronger, nonnegotiable tone was imperative in dialogue with Jovan.

To implement warm demander strategy of dialogue with Jovan, she decided to conduct interactions outside of the classroom space to limit the reactions an audience would engender. During these restorative dialogues, she intentionally excluded the concept of consequences. Rather, she chose to utilize the dialogue as a means to figure out the puzzle that was Jovan.

Ms. Bee was consistent with the practice of the 3 R's in her attempts to remediate Jovan's behaviors. While Ms. Bee did not experience a powerful breakthrough with Jovan, she observed that he did become less oppositional, which allowed for more dialogue to occur about his bullying and the expectations for student behavior within the classroom. On the occasions Jovan successfully regulated his behavior, his efforts met with positive reinforcement from Ms. Bee.

BE A WARM DEMANDER!

Ms. Bee's strategy of implementing warm demander pedagogy, (a) the cultivation of teacher-student relationships built on respect and trust, (b) the clear-cut communication of expectations of behavior, (c) the reminder of these expectations, (d) the repetition of these expectations, (e) the reinforcement of good behavior, and (f) the tone of insistence—respectful and caring, yet firm and unequivocal, proved to be a successful means to engage students previously disenfranchised and disillusioned with school.

In all four cases, the disruptive behaviors of the students decreased (see Figure 11.1). The warm demander techniques of insistence were easily incorporated into the daily classroom routine. The importance and significance of these student-teacher relationships built on trust and respect cannot be minimized.

Ms. Bee also discovered warm demander pedagogy to be sustainable as a pedagogical technique implemented over time as students do not eventually become sensitized, nor do they stop responding to the behavioral interventions. Once the establishment of personal relationships occurred, the *demanding* component to this pedagogy could then be implemented. The communication of nonnegotiable expectations and the insistence of appropriate behavior are critical to the success of the warm demander pedagogy.

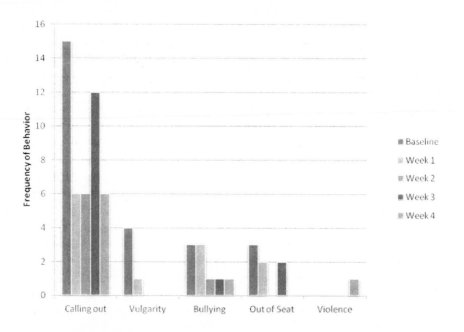

Figure 11.2.   Comparison of Baseline Behaviors and Behaviors During Warm Demander Intervention

Authors' Note

All names are pseudonyms.

REFERENCES

Bondy, E., Ross, D. D., Gallingame, C., & Hambacher, E. (2007). Creating environments of success and resilience: Culturally responsive classroom management and more. *Urban Education, 42*(4), 326–348. doi: 10.1177/0042085907303406

Hyland, N. E. (2009). One White teacher's struggle for culturally relevant pedagogy: The problem of the community. *The New Educator, 5*(2), 95–112. Retrieved from http://www1.ccny.cuny.edu/prospective/education/theneweducator/upload/1st-article-2.pdf

Ross, D. D., Bondy, E., Gallingame, C., & Hambacher, E. (2008). Promoting academic engagement through insistence: Being a warm demander. *Childhood Education, 84*(3), 142–146.

Ullucci, K. (2009). This has to be family: Humanizing classroom management in urban schools. *The Journal of Classroom Interaction, 44*(1), 13–28.

Chapter Twelve

Civil Talks: Logistics of Managing Online Classroom Spaces

Jeffrey P. Drake and Jeanette L. Drake

"*. . . thank you for saving me the trouble of Googling the word 'imbecile' because in my opinion that is what you clearly are.*"

This comment represents an educator's worst nightmare. It came from a random contributor in response to one student's blog that questioned whether the naming of a particular disease was a public relations stunt. The woman's son has the disease, so she wanted to set the blogger straight. She was not alone. Within hours, 38 responses were posted from across the country.

Steve, a high school teacher who requires his students to blog, had not anticipated this reaction. Unintended consequences are among the many challenges of managing online classroom spaces. Still, blogging about current issues remains a vibrant method for 21st century teachers because it provides constructivist learning in a democratic setting, and it aligns with Common Core Standards.

For social studies educators like Steve, online deliberative activities are worth the effort. As this chapter illustrates, however, that effort requires a new paradigm regarding classroom management embodied by Civil Talks, a process to prepare students to become responsible digital communicators.

INNOVATIVE ONLINE CLASSROOMS

Meet Nick, Tim, Steve, and Frank (all names are pseudonyms)—high school social studies teachers throughout the country who extend their lessons online and have discovered barriers and benefits of managing the virtual classroom. Their stories provide a glimpse into the nature of social studies blogging in high schools today and inform a new Model of Online Deliberation (Drake, 2012).

The model provides insights into managing online classroom spaces, which are categorized by varying degrees of *decisiveness* and by leanings toward *authenticity* or *proceduralism*, resulting in the online worksheet, bull session, seminar, debate, and deliberation. A focus on online reading and writing fits well under the Common Core umbrella, according to Kist (2013), who explained that:

> a primary thrust of the new standards is college and career readiness. How can we hope to prepare our young people to thrive in today's society—in which people are connected 24 hours a day by media and coworkers may well live in different countries—without giving them some practice with new media at school? (para. 4)

The teachers presented in this chapter recognize the alignment between media and real life practice.

BLOGGING FOR CONTENT KNOWLEDGE AND TECHNOLOGY SKILLS

Gunn and Hollingsworth (2013) have found a district-wide approach can have a significant influence on many factors, including the integration of technology in the classroom. Supporting this finding is Nick, who teaches at Roosevelt High School in a technology-rich suburban district in the South that gives all of its students and staff laptop computers. Using WordPress, he manages Nick's blog page for information dissemination, debate, and a repository of additional resources for his 11th grade American History class.

Nick ties historical controversies to topical discussions that students might find relevant. He designs counterfactual questions to give a historical debate currency, while at the same time covering content standards. For Nick, integrating new technologies is essential in meeting Common Core State Standards and making students career ready.

Resembling an *online worksheet*, this blog helps let Nick know if students are getting the facts right. Students show a high degree of decisiveness and a desire to follow the rules, especially in the beginning, often not disagreeing with peers and not displaying a great deal of authenticity in comments, as in this student's post about tea party symbols.

> I agree with both of your responses. Like you said, the first image does represent division of the colonies. They did want freedom from England. I like how you said it contrasts so greatly against how the colonists earlier intended it to be used.

Nick probes further when online participation becomes too rushed or per-functory. To manage the online space, Nick finds it helpful to require a specific number of posts from students each week and to allow comments to count for class participation. He limits the number of topics and waits for all posts to conclude before starting a new topic so the conversation does not become unwieldy. A three-point rubric helps keep grading manageable. He encourages more critical thinking as the year progresses and finds that asking students to reflect on the discussion stimulates deeper thinking.

BLOGGING FOR ONLINE SOCIAL SKILLS

Tim teaches ninth-grade Advanced Global Studies at Jackson High School, a small rural school in an eastern seaboard state. He created an online discussion site using Wikispaces that by default e-mails the teacher with site additions and comments. His ability to control the discussion is paramount to managing the online forum, as is the need to establish rules of engagement before getting started.

"It really has been a good way for [students] to practice having a critical conversation with each other," Tim says. "That's just part of a good social studies classroom. You try to go from just giving answers to having an actual dialogue." By focusing on social interaction, Tim's class wiki serves as an *online bull session*, as can be seen in excerpts about a Muslim center near Ground Zero. (All blog posts are presented as they appeared.)

> Tony: i feel like everyone is granted the right of freedom of religion, so technicly speaking they should be aloud to.

> Lusa: Tony why would you want this? All the things I looked up about this Muslim Cultural Center it says bad things about it & how it's going to put the Americcan troops in danger.If that's going to happen theres no reason to bulid it.

> Hattie: The muslims don't believe in bad things, Lusa.

> Alex: thats not always true hattie

"Some kids don't get it," Tim says. "They just become angry and they come in and won't talk with some person because they disagree with their post." Tim's assignment rationale of netiquette is evident on the blog and in his posted procedures, which underscore the importance of mutual respect, even during disagreement.

BLOGGING FOR AUTHENTICITY

Steve and Don co-teach 11th grade American Studies at Washington High School in an affluent Midwestern suburb. To manage their online classroom discussions, the teachers use Blogger so the technology does not overshadow the writing. Steve validates online activities in the classroom so students take them seriously. He finds that random, nonevaluative feedback often can fuel a discussion. Steve and Don also require students to develop and maintain their own blogs.

Steve describes their online classroom discussions as "mirrors that reflect American society." The teachers strive for an authentic blogging activity that models what they want their students to achieve—a more critical view of culture. The idea of influencing their peers and participating in emerging technologies is inherently motivating to students. One student, clearly a *screenager* (Rushkoff, 1996), continued posting well after the school year ended. She had over 8,000 readers on one post regarding her take on Amy Chua's (2011) controversial book about the *Tiger Mom*.

The in-depth exploration of controversial topics on the American Issues blog resembles an *online seminar*, as demonstrated by this excerpt from a 300-word student post addressing the role of education.

> One of the biggest ways to get students infused with "the substance of genuine learning" is to create an environment where risk taking (especially inserting a personal voice that might not go strictly along with the rubric) is encouraged. In schools around the country almost every assignment is given back to students with a final grade. This grade usually represents how well the student followed the rubric or memorized certain facts, but the grade discourages risk taking.

The online seminar is not necessarily concerned with decision making, but distinguishes itself with a high degree of authenticity and refined communication skills.

BLOGGING FOR AUTONOMY

Frank teaches 12th-grade AP Government at Hoover High School, an affluent suburban school in the Midwest. Using WordPress for his current issues blog, Frank collaborated with a class from a large inner-city neighborhood school taught by Drew for a month-long online deliberation about immigration. The teachers learned the value of extending class time for students to post, since Drew's students had difficulty accessing the Internet outside of school.

With a teaching rationale focusing on the students' autonomy, Frank works to develop critical thinking and literacy skills. Just as he does in the traditional classroom, Frank builds a sense of community online. His presence is obvious but not dominant. He models natural conversation and humor, and he draws students out in a nonthreatening way. Disagreement and diverse perspectives are common on this blog, which resembles an *online debate* with its rules-based competitive style and solid reasoning.

> Zach: . . . it's unfair to assume that just because an immigrant is here "illegally" that they are only a drain on the system. Many illegal immigrants do end up paying taxes to the government (an estimated $7 billion to Social Security).

The more students clashed, the more they cultivated their reasoning skills. At its finest, the discussion in this virtual classroom took on the nature of *online deliberation*, which occurs when the teacher balances authenticity and procedure, careful consideration and decisiveness.

BEST PRACTICES IN MANAGING ONLINE CLASSROOM SPACES

As teachers like Nick, Tim, Steve, and Frank know all too well, moving discussions to online spaces has necessitated new considerations for classroom management. Learning multiple new literacies is one such consideration, so, for example, these educators have added blogging lessons to their curriculum:

- Join the conversation. You might remind people of a previous discussion or begin with a compliment. Be positive, and be specific.
- Consider the audience. Even if you are responding to one other person directly, remember that the blogosphere is enormous and that you may have a much larger audience than a single reader.
- Pay attention. Answer the question asked. Look at previous comments to make sure no one has written what you want to say.
- Extend the conversation. Make sure your post does more than merely restate someone else's position. Add factual information.
- Play nice. Follow online etiquette and cite your sources.
- Stay current. Blogs must be relevant.
- Keep the conversation going. Ask relevant questions at the end of your comment.

In the online classroom, it is not surprising that students tend to mirror what the teacher models.

Jeffrey P. Drake and Jeanette L. Drake

The Evolution of Civil Talks

Civil Talks, a new four-phase process for building and managing the online classroom, was derived from extensive studies of issues blogging. Before using a blog as an online classroom space, however, teachers need to know and work within their school policies regarding the Internet, technology, and social media. It also is a good idea to create a policy for the blog and to make it public, sharing the policy and assessment strategies with students and parents in advance.

Phase I — Learn the rules and tools. It is important to take time in class to discuss how to blog but not to overwhelm students with the tools. Most important during this stage is helping students to understand the responsibility that comes with posting and the immediacy and permanence of posts. Teachers may wish to consider an acceptable use policy or class contract so expectations are clearly articulated. During the first phase, teachers review the school's safety, technology, and social media policies with students, discuss online communication etiquette, and obtain any necessary permission.

This is the time to determine the best content management system (CMS), assess students' technical knowledge, and provide training. Many teachers begin with the school's CMS and evolve to public forums. A variety of features help educators manage the online classroom, including privacy settings, editing options, and routing functions where posts go first to the teacher to decide if a post is suitable for publishing.

After aligning the platform and assignment to the learning context, teachers show students how to use the CMS, how to link and why, how to become efficient navigators in digital spaces, how to read web materials more effectively, how to critically engage media, and where to go for technology help.

Phase II — Learn and listen to deliberation. During the second phase, the teacher provides models of deliberative blogging such as the National Issues Forum (www.nifi.org) and the National Youth Rights Association (www.youthrights.org). Students should learn the importance of multiple perspectives, listening, open-mindedness, information and opinion give-and-take, and supporting evidence. To increase reasoning literacy, teachers may ask students to evaluate a discussion or use a flow sheet to outline opposing arguments (see Table 12.1). "Flowing" a debate is like taking a still photograph of an argument's structure for later evaluation.

Blogging plug-ins that allow comment rating systems help balance authentic blogging with necessary procedures and are easy to add. Intense Debate (intensedebate.com), one such web tool, allows users to rate comments on various website discussions. Students can join and rate conversations while having their own postings rated. The accumulation of points motivates students to engage authentically in criticism and to produce thoughtful comments.

Pro Case	Con Response	Con Case	Pro Response
Claim 1: Warrants (Proof): Impact (So what?):		Claim 1: Warrants (Proof): Impact (So what?):	
Claim 2: Warrants (Proof): Impact (So what?):		Claim 2: Warrants (Proof): Impact (So what?):	
Claim 3: Warrants (Proof): Impact (So what?):		Claim 3: Warrants (Proof): Impact (So what?):	

Table 12.1

Blank Flow Chart to Facilitate a Debate

Phase III — Practice, practice, practice. Establishing questions in a private online discussion is vital for nascent bloggers. To enhance students' deliberative skills and their dispositions of tolerance and open-mindedness, teachers can create procedures for students to argue both sides of an issue, for which ProCon (www.procon.org) provides an invaluable resource. Teachers may use the Model of Online Deliberation to follow the evolution of the class, beginning with an online worksheet or bull session and working their way toward online seminars, debates, and ideally, deliberations.

Phase IV — Own the issue and reflect. Educators have found social networking useful in helping students develop skills of deliberation (Beach & Doerr-Stevens, 2011). To do this, teachers must first define issues that are relevant to the classroom subject and to the students. Next, they must teach students to help monitor comments and play the role of *online civility cop*. Finally, teachers may decide to open the conversation to the public and be purposive in seeking diverse perspectives and reflection.

To augment cognitive opportunities, educators may incorporate reflective writing, online polling, reconsideration of a group decision, or service learning. Ultimately, teachers may help students manage their own online discussion sites.

CONCLUSION

With the Internet serving as the public square of the 21st century, digital citizenship education (ISTE, 2007) is a priority for educators, who must learn effective management strategies for online classroom spaces. Breaking new ground, Civil Talks and the Model of Online Deliberation (Drake, 2012) provide an incremental and innovative approach to creating and managing these online spaces. Social constructivism undergirds the practice (Doolittle & Hicks, 2003) and helps teachers facilitate civic dialogue online.

In fact, the nightmare at the beginning of this chapter became a needed lesson in civil dialogue, cyber conflict, and emotional growth, thanks to the teachers, Steve and Don, who treated it as a teachable moment and helped the student work through the situation via careful consideration, open dialogue, and ultimately, a public apology. This excerpt from the student's year-end blog post gives testament to the many lessons he learned.

> I was reminded that on the Internet, anything can be viewed by anyone . . . it can't be taken back . . . the impact an apology can have . . . the power of a controversial blog post can lead to good . . . general discussion . . . understand . . . show empathy.

REFERENCES

Beach, R., & Doerr-Stevens, C. (2011). Using social networking for online role-plays to develop students' argumentative strategies, *Journal of Educational Computing Research, 45*(2), 165–181.

Chua, A. (2011). *Battle hymn of the tiger mother.* New York, NY: Penguin.

Doolittle, P. E., & Hicks, D. (2003). Constructivism as a theoretical foundation for the use of technology in social studies. *Theory and Research in Social Education, 31*(1), 72–104.

Drake, J. P. (2012). *Civil talks: Analysis of online discussions in social studies classrooms.* (Unpublished doctoral dissertation). Kent State University, Kent, OH.

Gunn, T. M., & Hollingsworth, M. (2013). The implementation and assessment of a shared 21st century learning vision: A district-based approach. *Journal of Research on Technology in Education, 45*(3), 201–228.

ISTE (2007). *National educational technology standards and performance indicators for students.* Retrieved from http://www.iste.org/Content/NavigationMenu/NETS/ForStudents/2007Standards/NETS_for_Students_2007_Standards.pdf

Kist, W. (2013). New literacies and the common core. *Educational Leadership: Technology-rich Learning, 70*(6), 38–43. Retrieved from http://www.ascd.org/publications/educational-leadership/mar13/vol70/num06/New-Literacies-and-the-Common-Core.aspx

Rushkoff, D. (1996). *Playing the future: How kids' culture can teach us to think in an age of chaos.* New York, NY: HarperCollins.

Chapter Thirteen

Culturally Relevant Cyphers: Rethinking Classroom Management Through Hip-Hop–Based Education

Bettina L. Love

Hip-Hop–Based Education (HHBE) is youthful, energetic, rhythmic, impromptu, resourceful, and student-centered. At times it can be loud and fast-paced, combined with playful yet organic moments of skillful confrontation among students (known as battling). Its intent as an educational pedagogy is to create classroom experiences that are culturally relevant to students who embrace hip hop as their primary culture and discourse.

The five primary elements of hip-hop—MCing, Break dancing, Graffiti, Deejaying, and Knowledge of Self—embody how urban youth create, think, speak, move, and understand their surroundings inside and outside formal classroom settings (Love, 2012). Table 13.1 defines each element of hip-hop.

The foundation of HHBE is rooted in the critical teaching approaches of culturally relevant education (Ladson-Billings, 1995), critical pedagogical frameworks (Freire, 2000), and cultural modeling methods (Lee, 1995) to form a classroom that positions the culture, social context, learning styles, and student experiences at the center of the curricula. HHBE is more than just an educational teaching approach; it is also a classroom management style that promotes self-regulation, social-emotional learning, and community building.

The successful classroom management innovation highlighted within this chapter stems from an HHBE class called "Real Talk" at a local elementary school in Atlanta, Georgia. Over the course of 20 weeks, the class—comprising 17 fifth graders—met once a week for 90 minutes at a time. The class was part of a pilot project that examined how the elements of hip-hop could

Element	Definition
Rapping	The verbal art of expression through rhyming lyrics or spoken word
Breakdancing	An athletic, high-energy dance style set to the break or the beat patterns of hip hop music
Graffiti	Writings, drawings, or tags inscribed on walls or public buildings
Deejaying	The use of music to set the tone, to educate, and to excite party goers
Knowledge of self	The study of hip-hop culture, music, and elements, alongside examining issues within one's surroundings, to create positive change in one's community

Table 13.1 *The Five Elements of Hip Hop*

be linked to the Common Core State Standards (NGA/CCSSO, 2010) through the students' formal school curriculum.

CLASSROOM MANAGEMENT AND HHBE

One of the overall goals of Real Talk was to examine hip-hop's effectiveness as a pedagogical framework for developing reading, writing, as well as scientific and critical thinking skills with elementary-aged urban learners. The project also investigated the classroom management styles developed through the pedagogical method of HHBE.

In that vein, the teachers were concerned with how the classroom structure of Real Talk promoted student engagement. A close examination was made of classroom activities that were culturally relevant and encouraged student self-regulation, social-emotional learning, and community building.

The Cypher

One signature dimension of the hip-hop–structured "Morning Meeting" was the cypher. A cypher is "a circle of energy ignited by a community as they express artistic ideas" (Livaudais, 2008, p. 56). As a youth-centered space created by the emotional intensity of participants, cyphers allow students and teachers to challenge and learn from each other. Similar to a Morning Meeting, the cyphers comprised four elements: greeting, sharing, group activity, and the message of the day. Students participated in the cypher at the beginning of each Real Talk class once a week. As a classroom management strategy, a cypher set the tone for classroom instruction by

• laying the foundation for each lesson;

- greeting students in culturally affirming customs;
- creating a space for students to share their experiences;
- cultivating a space to establish students' trust; and
- promoting social skills of cooperation, self-control, empathy, and love.

Tying into the concepts discussed above, restructuring (remixing) the Morning Meeting to reflect students' hip-hop culture increased student engagement and established new expectations for successful classroom management.

Cultural Circles

Similar to Freire's (2002) cultural circles, cyphers function as spaces to help students, "clarify situations or seek action arising from that clarification" (p. 42). In offering that definition, the teachers of Real Talk understood that learners need safe and trusting spaces to create action for social change.

Historically, hip-hop educators have utilized Freirean-style "critical cultural cyphers" (Petchauer, 2009, p. 953) to place the realities of students' lives at the center of the classroom. Thus, cyphers enable students to "revise and reconstruct their thought processes about topics and their own lives" (Petchauer, p. 953) and promote critical consciousness.

MORE THAN JUST A MEETING: RECOGNIZING AND AFFIRMING CULTURE

Drawing on the work of critical cultural cyphers, Real Talk utilized the technique as a cultural space for students to discuss issues that impacted their lives, but also to help students understand the norms and rules of the classroom in ways similar to Morning Meetings. Traditionally, Morning Meetings provide an intentional space for students to practice greetings, listening and responding skills, and group problem solving (Kriete & Bectel, 2002).

According to Kriete and Bectel (2002), Morning Meetings give students the opportunity to learn to take care of themselves and other students, while learning the social skills of respectful behavior and community building. However, most Morning Meetings are teacher-centered and do not reflect students' culture, especially that of urban students who identify with hip-hop culture.

Morning Meetings should teach students to listen, keep their bodies in control, raise their hands to talk, keep their hands down when someone else is speaking, and not laugh at individuals in the circle (Kriete & Bectel, 2002). That traditional structure of a Morning Meeting ignores and devalues urban students' culture.

While the rationale for using cyphers in the classroom is rooted in the culture of urban students who identify with hip-hop, this innovative classroom management strategy is also grounded in Culturally Responsive Classroom Management (CRCM). Weinstein, Tomlinson-Clarke, and Curran (2004) emphasized that CRCM reflects the importance of self-regulation, community building, and social decision making.

CULTURALLY RESPONSIVE CLASSROOM MANAGEMENT (REMIXED)

Culturally Responsive Classroom Management provides a framework for teachers to (a) consider their ethnocentrism and biases, (b) learn about their students' cultural backgrounds, (c) develop a greater awareness of the broader social, economic, and political contexts that impact students' lives, (d) curate an ability and willingness to use culturally appropriate management strategies, and (e) commit to building caring classroom communities. CRCM helps teachers understand the worldviews, communication patterns, and customs of their students, as both students and teachers experience the importance of community building.

As a classroom organizational approach rooted in the tenets of CRCM, HHBE is fundamentally concerned with teaching youth to examine their lived spaces for the purpose of community building. By teaching the five elements of hip-hop, educators reach students through their own cultural knowledge and talents.

Reframing Discipline

Real Talk utilized hip-hop's customs and rituals to structure the classroom in ways that affirmed students' learning styles to create culturally appropriate management strategies. For example, students speaking out of turn was not perceived as a disruption, but rather valued as an energetic, impromptu response to learning. Similarly, rapping, bobbing their heads, or beating on their desks in a rhythmic fashion in order to learn a concept was encouraged and not viewed as a punishable offense.

Rather than focusing on preventing cheating, the classroom structure encouraged and celebrated students working together to produce knowledge-building activities. Finally, and most important, Real Talk centered on students understanding of how their behavior—positive or negative—impacted their community.

According to Weinstein, et al. (2004), culturally responsive teaching requires teachers to learn the cultural norms, beliefs, and the ways in which students' culture considers time and space. Morning Meetings are a powerful space for students to take personal interest in their education and learn from their peers. However, it is counterproductive to ask students to emotionally open up, while simultaneously ignoring their ways of doing so. Moreover, the traditional structure of a Morning Meeting marginalizes urban youth because it asks them to follow mainstream sociocultural norms, and places their culture at the borders of the classroom, at best.

PUTTING THEORY INTO PRACTICE: CULTURALLY RELEVANT CYPHERS

Each Real Talk session began with a cypher. Each greeting represented aspects of hip-hop culture or African American traditions. For example, students greeted each other with culturally familiar phrases that they value, such as "What's Up Fam?" and "Two Times." When someone greets an urban youth by saying, "What's Up Fam?" he or she is implying that they are more than friends, they are family.

Fictional family members are a spirited and long-standing ritual of African American culture as a way to build community outside the immediate family. After the class greeted each other in that way, they discussed how family is an important aspect to creating a loving school environment. The greeting "Two Times" is a handshake that shows solidarity.

Baugh (1999) contended that handshakes are symbols of personal relationships and one way in which African Americans, especially males, express themselves. Sharing is also a significant part of a cypher. However, sharing is self-regulated by the emotion of the cypher. Youth who are participating in a cypher internally and intuitively know when it is their turn to participate.

Entering the Cypher: Student Synergy

During a cypher, it is rare for students to raise their hands or ask to speak. Their participation is determined by the synergy of the circle. Thus, students learn how to self-regulate by understanding the emotions of their classmates, which is much more powerful than waiting for someone to finish speaking. To enter a cypher, students must listen to their classmates in order to relate to their point of view and not only contribute to, but also enhance, the cypher. Group activities are always filled with movement, energy, and elements of hip-hop culture. Activities, just like the message of the day, inform students about the lesson or theme of the day.

For an example of the interplay between the key elements of a cypher, one lesson explored the history of breakdancing and how elements of physics (force, momentum, and velocity) can be applied to the dance form. The greeting of that day was "Let's Battle." The students were asked to share what they thought this idiom meant in hip-hop culture.

Members of the class discussed how battling in hip-hop has nothing to do with violence and everything to do with showcasing one's talents. Next, through a group activity, the students showed the class their best hip-hop moves. Last, the message of the day was "Dance is Art." The message set the tone for the day as students learned that dance is an art form just like painting, creating music, and acting. Through this lesson, Real Talk integrated hip-hop into the formal curriculum, while valuing how students culturally learn and live as *Hiphopas*.

LET'S BUILD

Classroom management can either promote or impede learning. A fundamental part of teaching lies in understanding how to build community in a classroom. However, classroom management is damaging if students are managed in ways that devalue their culture and how they learn. Thus, classroom management must take up the work of community building. Students' culture and the ways in which they learn are key to creating classrooms where students feel valued, respected, and trusted to be good stewards of their own education.

Real Talk started each weekly class and created a space for students to enjoy and learn more about their culture, while practicing notions of self-regulation and social-emotional learning through a well-known hip-hop ritual. In that way, Real Talk placed students' cultural norms and learning styles at the center of classroom management, thereby transforming it into a microcosm of community building.

REFERENCES

Baugh, J. (1999). *Out of the mouths of slaves: African American language and educational malpractice.* Austin, TX: University of Texas Press.
Freire, P. (2000). *Pedagogy of the oppressed.* New York, NY: Continuum.
Freire, P. (2002). *Education for critical consciousness.* New York, NY: Continuum.
Kriete, R., & Bectel, L. (2002). *The Morning Meeting book.* Greenfield, MA: Northeast Foundation for Children.
Ladson-Billings, G. (1995). But that's just good teaching! The case for culturally relevant pedagogy. *Theory into Practice, 34,* 159–165. doi: 10.1080/00405849509543675
Lee, C. D. (1995). Signifying as a scaffold for literary interpretation. *Journal of Black Psychology, 21,* 357–381. doi: 10.1177/00957984950214005
Livaudais, S. (2008, July). Austin's hip-hop project. *The Good Life,* 52–58.
Love, B. L. (2012). *Hip hop's li'l sistas speak: Negotiating identities and politics in the new south.* New York, NY: Peter Lang.
National Governors Association Center for Best Practices (NGA)/Council of Chief State School Officers (CCSSO). (2010). *Common Core State Standards for ELA, literacy in history/social studies, science, and technical subjects.* Retrieved from http://www .corestandards.org/assets/CCSSI_ELA%20Standards.pdf

Petchauer, E. (2009). Framing and reviewing hip-hop educational research. *Review of Educational Research, 79*, 946–978. doi: 10.3102/0034654308330967

Weinstein, C., Tomlinson-Clarke, S., & Curran, M. (2004). Toward a conception of culturally responsive classroom management. *Journal of Teacher Education, 55*(1), 25–38. doi: 10.1177/0022487103259812

Chapter Fourteen

Flipping the Cultural Revolution

Jon Nordmeyer and Peter Stelzer

A visitor walking into a ninth-grade Asian History class at Shanghai American School during our three-week unit on the Cultural Revolution would see students engaged in a variety of activities:

Simon, a 14-year-old Japanese student, is preparing to meet with Mr. Stelzer to present an oral summary of the 1950s Chinese propaganda video he watched the night before. As he waits for class to begin, he goes over to his folder to see how many unit points he still needs, and decides what task he wants to do next.

Sophie and Vanessa, two students from Korea, are already at their desks. They are focused on the task: "Have a discussion with another student, in English or another language; imagine what would happen at Shanghai American School if [high school principal] Dr. Borden started his own Cultural Revolution." Both girls share their ideas in Korean and Sophie takes notes in English on her laptop.

Min Kyung is putting the finishing touches on a speech she will give to the class. She has dressed up and will be speaking as a member of Chairman Mao's Red Guards, young people her age who formed the vanguard of the Cultural Revolution. The independent project that she designed is a speech to be given to her classmates justifying her involvement with a Red Guard brigade that destroyed a store selling Western goods. At home she watched Mr. Stelzer's videos about the Red Guard and interviewed the school librarian, whose sister was a Red Guard member who participated in similar actions.

As a history teacher and an English as an Additional Language (EAL) teacher, we incorporated two complementary approaches to organizing content and classroom activity—flipping and layered choice—which supported both effective student learning *and* efficient management of this ninth-grade

111

Asian history class. This chapter offers a narrative account of how this unit was organized, the benefits of utilizing these innovative approaches, and a reflection on why we think this technique resulted in effective classroom management and authentic learning.

AN AMERICAN SCHOOL IN THE MIDDLE KINGDOM

Shanghai American School, the largest international school in China, is a private, independent school with 3,000 pre-K through grade 12 students. English is the language of instruction and the school offers a challenging, college preparatory curriculum, including both Advanced Placement courses and the International Baccalaureate Diploma. Curriculum and instruction reflect current trends in North American education, such as standards-based assessment.

In addition, both the middle school and high school have implemented a 1:1 laptop program over the past five years, and all teachers use some form of a complementary online learning tool, ranging from simple blogs to interactive wikis or Moodles. Classrooms in the school are diverse, both linguistically and culturally, with targeted support for English language learners and students with learning differences.

Students come from a variety of countries in Asia, Europe, and North America. Almost all students are bilingual, with Mandarin Chinese speakers being the largest language group. Overall, the students tend to have strong educational backgrounds, with parents who are successful in the global workforce.

NUTS AND BOLTS: HOW IT WORKED

This three-week Cultural Revolution unit was the culmination of students' examination of life in Mao's China. Learning targets were established and intended to build the skills and knowledge necessary for students to analyze the events of the period 1966–1974 in China.

We "flipped" this unit by requiring students to view teacher-generated video clips outside of class to provide background on the Cultural Revolution. The students were familiar with this approach, as previous units had established the use of video lectures. We wrote and recorded videos consisting primarily of narrated slideshows using Screenflow for Mac software, uploaded to the school's server, where they could be viewed on any Internet-enabled device as well as downloaded directly by the student. Each 10–12 minute video lecture had accompanying guided questions.

In addition to required video comprehension checks in class, students were given a wide variety of *layered* options for learning activities connected to one of the unit's enduring understandings (Nunley, 2004). In order to accomplish these tasks, we provided students with a number of resources they could use: websites, textbooks, documentary video excerpts, and primary source accounts of the events in question.

We designed activity choices for visual, auditory, and tactile learners and included, for example, giving speeches, moderating group discussions, debating ideas with classmates, listening to podcasts, preparing vocabulary lists, and interpreting document-based primary sources. Each activity was assigned a number of points depending upon its difficulty, complexity, and approximate length of time for completion.

Students could repeat certain activities, for example retaking an oral vocabulary quiz, as their understanding increased. Although students were responsible for demonstrating specific skills and knowledge by the end of the unit, the students themselves decided what activities to pursue and in what order. After successful completion of activities, students gave an oral explanation of their work product. For example, students explained why they chose particular images for original propaganda posters and how the images reinforced the "Cult of Mao" and utilized propaganda techniques.

During class we met with individuals and groups to monitor and advise activity choices, offering next steps, and checking understanding. We answered questions and discussed key concepts. When students were ready to be assessed, they presented an innovative, student-created product or engaged in an oral defense to demonstrate understanding.

The unit culminated in two activities requiring higher-level thinking on Bloom's taxonomy. First, students interviewed someone who lived through the Cultural Revolution and wrote a summary and personal reflection of what they learned. As a summative assessment, students had to incorporate information from both this and earlier units to address the overarching essential question: "Was Mao good for China?" As with the rest of the unit, students chose one of several ways to answer this question.

FLIPPING THE CLASSROOM: WHY IT WORKED

In its most basic format, flipping a classroom is a way to time-shift direct instruction; content that is usually delivered during a traditional class is accessed by students at home, through teacher-created lectures or other web-based videos or podcasts. As a result, class time can be used for higher order thinking activities.

> The value of a flipped class is in the repurposing of class time into a workshop where students can inquire about lecture content, test their skills in applying knowledge, and interact with one another in hands-on activities. During class

sessions, instructors function as coaches or advisors, encouraging students in individual inquiry and collaborative effort. (Educause, 2012, p. 1)

We found that a flipped/layered approach to teaching the Cultural Revolution led to a more active, engaged student population. Effective class management was supported by instruction that allowed greater student choice, gave clear expectations, encouraged student responsibility for learning, and utilized interesting, real-life assignments and assessments. In reflecting on this unit, several themes emerged: the importance of choice, changing roles, differentiation, and building community.

Student Choice

The important notion of allowing student choice significantly contributed to the unit's success. Within general guidelines, students pursued their interests, chose when and in what way they would learn, and decided how to demonstrate learning. Students had the luxury of pausing, rewinding, and watching content multiple times for clarity or review, and came to class more prepared, informed, and immediately engaged by in-class activities.

Whether they watched content videos on their iPad on the bus or their laptop at home, students had control over the time and location of their own learning. Students were no longer bored, disengaged *captive learners*. Ultimately, whether they demonstrated understanding of Mao's political philosophy by analyzing a series of Mao quotes, writing a two-paragraph explanation, or giving a speech, students were able to integrate their understanding with their skills.

Students who liked to make videos, write historical fiction, or analyze a multifaceted picture with a political message all had opportunities to do so. No two students followed the same path. The flipped and layered approach put responsibility for learning where we believe it must be—in students' hands—and encouraged them to be energetic, informed, and responsible learners.

Independence and Responsibility

Our approach to organizing the unit also had a dynamic impact on classroom management. The typical challenges of maintaining students' attention were minimized as, in many ways, the classroom managed itself. This was true because students soon recognized that *they* had to manage themselves. On both a daily and continuing basis, students had to plan what activities to pursue and how to logically sequence them.

At the beginning of class, students either checked their project folder to review points or continued with ongoing projects. During class they worked independently or in small groups and, when ready, "signed up" with us for review and assessment. For homework, students knew to watch or review videos or continue with unit activities.

We established routines with which students quickly became accustomed. Students had ownership of this procedure because they had control over it. Every student knew exactly what the learning targets were and how to meet or exceed them. This accountability and transparency fostered an ongoing, positive class atmosphere.

The flipped and layered approach also sidelined the recurring issue of student absences. Missing class had little or no impact on student learning; videos could be watched and assignments completed from almost any location. No longer was a student significantly hindered because he or she missed a critical lecture or class discussion. We were relieved that at no time during the unit did a student approach and say: "I missed last class . . . what did we do?"

Changing Roles and Differentiating Instruction

Our role and responsibilities as instructors also shifted. We were no longer a *sage on the stage,* instead we became a *guide on the side.* We spent the majority of class with individuals or small groups answering questions, clarifying concepts, providing feedback, and evaluating assessments. We could also suggest creative, alternative activities as appropriate. For example, the independent project of a student named Justin came about when he asked about the words to Red Guard marching songs.

Because Justin was in a student rock band, we offered him additional points if he researched, wrote, and performed in class a song that mirrored those actually sung by Red Guards. Justin readily agreed, and his performance was one of the unit's highlights.

Changing both student and teacher roles naturally led to differentiation. As a history teacher and an EAL specialist, an explicit goal of our collaboration was to identify which students needed more scaffolding and provide appropriate support. For example, if students needed to revise an activity or repeat an assessment, we provided clear feedback on how they could reach learning targets. Likewise, we determined which students could benefit from extended learning activities.

Additionally, the resources we provided for students varied in level of difficulty and modality. Students could preview and select the most appropriate resources, according to their English language proficiency or learning style. For example, students might choose between a text-based article, a video, or a slideshow with text and images. If students accessed different source materials from a classmate, they were able to share different key ideas or historical details.

Finally, content was also differentiated because students could choose to watch a more difficult video several times to ensure comprehension. With input from the teacher, each learner followed a unique pathway. Based on common learning targets, students worked largely independently during class and received individualized instruction revolving around concepts or activities they chose; as a result, student engagement was noticeably increased.

Classroom as Community

An important aspect of managing this unit was building classroom community. Since many of the in-class activities required a partner or small group, students worked together to apply ideas, check their understanding, and demonstrate their learning. This positive interdependence is essential for cooperative learning and helps students to see peers as valuable resources in the learning process (Kagan, 2009).

We also built community through home-school connections. Because the majority of our students' families had strong ties to China, teaching about the many changes in the past century was not only relevant but personal. Many students had parents or grandparents who were directly impacted by the Chinese government's policies during the Cultural Revolution and brought a wealth of background knowledge and varying perspectives on the historical events of the 20th century in China.

Building the home-school connection helped to engage students both in class and at home. For example, students conducted interviews, which became an extremely powerful learning activity. Many students encountered family histories that they had no knowledge of previously. Several parents commented that these conversations with their children were memorable and surprising. Some students' family members had been purged and had suffered great hardship. Others were Red Guard members—young people who formed the vanguard of Mao's loyalist troops and participated in activities that reflected the chaos and violence of the times.

For students who did not have Chinese relatives, living in China made finding an appropriate interview subject relatively straightforward. By tapping into the larger community as resources, we were able to enrich the study of history and create primary source material for students to share with the class.

REFLECTIONS: WHY FLIPPING SUPPORTS 21ST CENTURY CLASSROOMS

In designing this unit, we recognized that 21st century students are operating in a new *learnscape* (Cross, 2007) that is very different from classrooms when we, the current generation of teachers, went to school. In many cases, students are more knowledgeable than their teachers about using 21st century information tools. By utilizing technology that allowed students to connect with each other and individualize their own learning experience, this unit on the Cultural Revolution was collaborative, creative, and complex.

The time-shift of the flipped classroom provided more time for individual, pair, and small group work within the class. Providing a variety of layered options within a defined curricular framework resulted in class activity that was differentiated, interactive, and meaningful. Students were active learners and, as teachers, we found ourselves responding to questions rather than monitoring students or keeping them on task.

When we flipped this unit, students learned to appreciate themselves, their classmates, and their families as valuable resources. By choosing how they would access content at home, they were in control of their learning process. Because of the interactive nature of classroom activities, students relied on peers to complete activities.

Choosing from a variety of assessment options, students proudly provided evidence of their learning, whether explaining how a quote from Mao Zedong connected to George Orwell's (1946/1996) allegorical novel *Animal Farm* or relating a parent's oral history to the Cultural Revolution. We found that the community formed in the classroom supported a diverse group of learners, and allowed us to not only facilitate, but also enjoy our students' learning along the way.

REFERENCES

Cross, J. (2007). *Designing a web-based learning ecology.* Retrieved from http://www.informl.com/2007/01/18/designing-a-web-based-learning-ecology/

Educause. (2012). *Things you should know about™ . . . Flipped classrooms.* Retrieved from http://net.educause.edu/ir/library/pdf/eli7081.pdf

Kagan, S. (2009). *Kagan cooperative learning* (2nd ed.). San Clemente, CA: Kagan.

Nunley, K. (2004). *Layered curriculum: The practical solution for teachers with more than one student in their classroom* (2nd ed.). Amherst, NH: Brains.org.

Orwell, G. (1946/1996). *Animal farm.* New York, NY: Plume.

Chapter Fifteen

Promoting Mutual Respect and Democratic Practice in Diverse Learning Communities to Foster Positive Classroom Management

Jennifer Lauria

"I don't know how teachers can handle this every single day. It seems like they need to constantly yell, scold, and threaten students with disciplinary measures just to get any of the children to listen and pay attention. These students are impossible and I'm exhausted after only three days!" (Graduate student teacher [MSED-Childhood: 1–6]).

Impressionable teacher candidates have expressed similar concerns about classroom management. It is no surprise that classroom management often is cited as a reason for leaving the teaching profession and is a legitimate source of anxiety for those preparing to become educators. It took less than one week for the graduate student teacher quoted above to discover that it was not "impossible children," but rather, lack of an effective classroom management system that was the root of the problem in his unpleasant student teaching environment.

Fortunately, he learned to implement key strategies to help him avoid common and unsuccessful management problems in diverse and inclusive classrooms in the future. This student teacher's challenges were not unique. Teacher candidates often express disappointment and frustration in response to certain classroom management strategies, or lack thereof, witnessed in some school placements. The dialogue that emerges among candidates, faculty, cooperating teachers, and supervisors results in recognition of best practices, many of which embody a crucial element—mutual respect that encompasses genuine caring and trust.

When student learners begin to appreciate their own value in the academic environment, they tend to work harder because they sense that their teachers believe in them. Even low-performing students with poor attitudes toward school can respond to a caring and respectful approach in the classroom. Some do not realize they can do well in school because they may have never been made to feel success is attainable. More challenging students might even express that they are not going to do anything they are told to do. The phrase *told to do* signals that they do not feel like stakeholders in the classroom management system.

When students feel valued as learning community members and understand the need for rules and procedures that maintain order and safety that support learning, they are less likely to rebel. Educators can establish this dynamic by including the students in the development of the classroom rules and empowering learners to make good choices, and ultimately, become responsible for those choices. For instance, activities such as role-playing, discussing real-life examples, polling students' opinions, and gathering input through surveys are methods for eliciting suggestions from students to increase ownership of the classroom management system.

Naturally, these elements take time and patience to develop, but are well worth the effort due to the decreased loss of learning time going forward when smooth procedures are established. The democratic approach to careful consideration of students' input and feedback allows students to perceive themselves as valued members of the learning community and to become true stakeholders. For many students, particularly learners regularly disciplined for behavioral infractions, the concept of having a stake in the classroom management system and feeling their opinions are valued by teachers and classmates is a foreign concept.

Many students will thrive when they feel they have had some input regarding the learning environment. Additionally, teachers can begin to develop rapport with students by sharing a little bit about themselves and asking students to share the same in return through individual interest questionnaires, journal writing, and discussion in an effort to get to know one another. Connecting with learners in this manner helps to convince them to put forth their best efforts.

INHERENT ELEMENTS OF SUCCESSFUL CLASSROOM MANAGEMENT SYSTEMS

The consistent plea from student teachers asking, "How should I manage my classroom?" leads teacher educators to reflect back on the very same challenges they once faced as novices. The basic, yet crucial element that made all the difference in those early teaching days was the emergence of mutual respect within the learning community, built upon caring and trust, and supported by time and patience. As depicted in Figure 15.1, all three essential factors necessary for successful classroom management are interdependent.

A caring disposition fosters the development of trust, which in turn supports the emergence of mutual respect in the classroom. Once mutual respect is established, students tend to want to work harder and make better choices out of growing respect for themselves, their peers, and teachers. Roache (2011) reported on the evolving body of research supporting the need for the student-teacher relationship to be built on a basis of sensitivity, trust, and mutual respect.

Without genuine caring, trust, and mutual respect, all members of a classroom and school-wide learning community miss out on the magic that can transpire when members value one another in a democratic learning environment and authentic learning can begin to blossom and flourish.

In environments devoid of the essence of caring, there is no chance for success in creating an authentic, stimulating learning community that values its members. Children are emotionally attuned to recognize caring, or lack thereof, and they seek and thrive in environments where it is present (Elias et

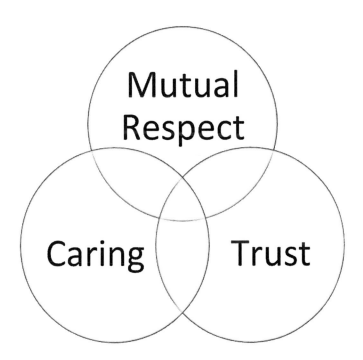

Figure 15.1.   Key Characteristics for Successful Classroom Management Systems

al., 1997). Genuine caring about the well-being of learners is absolutely vital to high-quality teaching and the ultimate goal of maximizing students' learning potential.

In the absence of effective classroom management systems that infuse caring and trust to develop the ultimate goal of mutual respect, significant learning time is lost throughout the day. The resultant sacrifice of valuable time leads to a slew of related problems, such as lack of deep, authentic learning and insufficient mastery of knowledge, skills, and standards needed as essential building blocks for future learning. The daily instances of lost learning time due to lack of effective management routines multiplied by days per school week, month, and year amount to a staggering and unnecessary sacrifice of learning time due to classroom management obstacles.

Use of effective classroom management techniques that promote mutual respect can support educators in avoiding unnecessary loss of learning time. A commonly misunderstood term, classroom management, is often considered a synonym for discipline. Unfortunately, with this interpretation in mind, discipline becomes the primary focus instead of learning (Wong, Wong, Rogers, & Brooks, 2012). A more accurate definition of classroom management was offered by Willis (2012) as an attitude and sense of confidence that needs to become intuitive.

Wong et al. (2012) described a classroom management system as procedures that create an environment that is safe, trusting, caring, and that benefit the students. The essence of mutual respect and an inherent tone of valuing others in a learning community help to create a classroom and school-wide environment in which, ideally, students desire to do their best, challenge themselves, trust and respect others, and participate meaningfully.

Respectful classroom management techniques that value each individual's contributions to the learning community, while acknowledging students' target areas for improvement in supportive, communicative ways, foster the development of mutual respect and thoughtful communication. Lauria and Preskill (2011) described treating everyone as valued and appreciated members of the learning community as an essential component of democratic practice.

Collaboration and effective communication can flourish when students, especially struggling students accustomed to nonconstructive and often unprofessional criticism, feel respected. Praise is earned and perceived as meaningful. Feedback is effective due to its specific and immediate focus in context. A most pleasant turn of events tends to occur, in time, in this type of democratic learning environment (Lauria & Preskill, 2011). The essence of mutual respect that infuses the classroom creates a dynamic in which the respect the teacher consistently demonstrated toward the students over time comes back to them exponentially.

Administrators and seasoned educators alike often suggest that novice teachers focus primarily on policies and procedures at the start of the school year and urge them to remain steadfast with consistency and patience. Many novice teachers are pleasantly surprised, and a bit shocked too, when they discover that such a simple approach works so well. They come to realize the need to be very firm instructional leaders, but also kind and respectful at the same time.

Lemove (2010) suggested one of many classroom management techniques labeled *warm/strict*, which demonstrates how "teachers must be both: caring, funny, warm, concerned, and nurturing—and also strict, by the book, relentless, and sometimes inflexible" (p. 213). Additionally, he stressed the need for balance in combining *warm* behaviors (being positive, enthusiastic, caring, and thoughtful) and *strict approaches* (being clear, consistent, firm, and unrelenting) to help students internalize contradictions and work through them.

THE ROAD TO MUTUAL RESPECT BEGINS WITH CARING AND TRUST

The road to developing a classroom management system that promotes mutual respect can be traveled one step at a time. The essential elements educators need to establish on this journey are outlined in Figure 15.2. Each of the components is interrelated and supports the development of caring and trust in a democratic learning community toward the ultimate goal of mutual respect.

Target Behaviors

Teachers working toward the goal of establishing mutual respect can begin by taking small steps, such as modeling target behaviors, including demonstration of the use of respectful language, good manners, and reflective discussion skills focused on consideration of multiple viewpoints in conversation. Indicating curiosity about students' individual interests helps build rapport with students and begins to create a sense of caring in the classroom. When the teacher is aware of students' learning preferences, they will feel valued.

Clear Communication

Establish clear rules, consequences, and expectations right from the start. Incorporating student input through creative discussion techniques—when developing rules and consequences—helps to create common ground among diverse stakeholders. Once in place, it is important to share expectations with

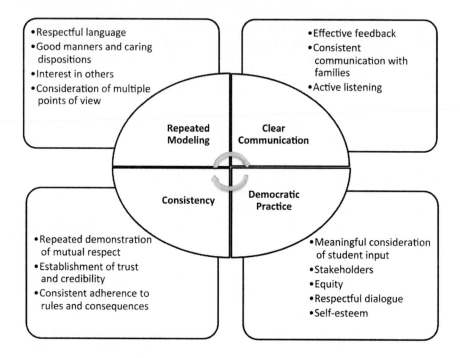

Figure 15.2.   Essential Elements of Respectful Classroom Management Systems

families and build a strong home-school connection. Students are less likely to misbehave and are more likely to become academically engaged if they know teachers are communicating directly with their families. Teachers should communicate expectations effectively and consistently.

Students need to feel like valued stakeholders in order to support the classroom management system. After collaboratively developing the classroom rules and consequences, it is helpful to have students sign the classroom rules poster as coauthors of the system and display it prominently, with the students' signatures serving as gentle reminders of the collaboration and need for making responsible choices in the classroom.

Learners will be more likely to abide by the rules when they are not imposed upon them, but rather because their input was carefully considered. As a result of these opportunities for clear communication, students are more likely to understand why certain measures need to be in place to maintain a safe and orderly learning environment.

EFFECTIVE FEEDBACK

Whenever teacher input is required—regarding instances of achievement, attitudes, behavior, work habits, or socialization—feedback must be specific and immediate. Collaborative evaluations, such as writing conferences and one-to-one assessments, also provide opportunities for teachers to share clear communication of effective detailed feedback.

Consistency

If you say you are going to do something, do it! Be careful with word choice and avoid idle threats. Students need to learn early on that their teacher's word means something significant in order to establish trust and credibility. Each time an instructional leader chooses not to be consistent in implementation of the classroom management system, they decrease the value of their word in the students' eyes. Consistency is vital to successful classroom management.

Patience

One can never have too much patience, but too little is a recipe for disaster in the classroom. It is essential to remain focused on the target result and to remember that it will take time for all elements of a classroom management system to run smoothly.

Democratic Practice

Creating an equitable climate where all students' voices can be heard, including divergent opinions, is crucial to the development of mutual respect within a community of learners. Students need to feel a sense of belonging and respect within the classroom and the schoolwide learning community. Teachers must model democratic dispositions and behaviors for students to emulate.

Self-Esteem

It is important for students to have ample opportunities for the ongoing development of self-esteem. If students' levels of self-esteem increase as a result of feeling good intrinsically about making positive choices rather than relying on extrinsic praise and rewards for demonstrating target behavior, they might not need or desire as many extrinsic supports to influence behavior and work ethic. A key factor about use of rewards in the classroom in response to appropriate behaviors is that teachers need to ensure that students do not view them as forms of coercion, but rather as healthy motivators (Marzano, Gaddy, Foseid, Foseid, & Marzano, 2005).

CONCLUSION

Educators should not underestimate the power of caring, trust, and mutual respect, along with democratic practice, in creating classroom management systems that empower diverse students to make good choices and, as stakeholders, demonstrate responsibility for those choices in the classroom. Fostering the development of mutual respect within the learning community through modeling of caring dispositions and encouragement of trust will support students' abilities to apply related habits of mind in their lives outside of school in the local and global community.

The path toward becoming caring, responsible, productive global citizens begins with successful participation in an academic learning community. Positive experiences in school that allow learners to work toward their maximal potential are shaped by the classroom management systems teachers employ and, therefore, it is imperative that educators carefully consider management techniques that promote mutual respect among all stakeholders.

REFERENCES

Elias, M., Zins, J., Weissberg, R., Frey, K., Greenberg, M., Haynes, N., et al. (1997). *Promoting social and emotional learning.* Alexandria, VA: ASCD.

Lauria, J., & Preskill, S. (2011). Building, promoting, and supporting successful hybrid online learning communities: Practical applications for effective collaboration from an accredited New York City teacher education program. *Excelsior: Leadership in Teaching and Learning, 6*(1), 41–55.

Lemove, D. (2010). *Teach like a champion.* San Francisco, CA: John Wiley & Sons.

Marzano, R., Gaddy, B., Foseid, M. C., Foseid, M. P., & Marzano, J. (2005). *A handbook for classroom management that works.* Alexandria, VA: ASCD.

Roache, J. (2011). Teachers' views on the impact of classroom management on student responsibility. *Australian Journal of Education, 55,* 132–146.

Willis, C. (Winter/Spring 2012). Being unprepared in order to be prepared: Intuitive classroom management and community formation. *Ohio Journal of English Language Arts, 52*(1), 39–42.

Wong, H., Wong, R., Rogers, K., & Brooks, A. (2012). Managing your classroom for success. *Science and Children, 49*(9), 60–64.

Chapter Sixteen

Classroom Management Strategies to Increase Student Collaboration

Maria G. Dove and Vicky Giouroukakis

In a New York suburban middle school, Ms. Malone begins a social studies lesson with her seventh graders. The room is extremely quiet, and the teacher assures that it will stay that way by keeping the students seated in straight rows and writing the names of offenders on the board. She calmly reminds students of the consequences for not adhering to her rules—an initial warning followed by a phone call home if the offense is repeated.

Students in Ms. Malone's class tend to settle down quickly and begin to independently complete the daily assignment as written on the board. For the rest of the lesson, she displays printed text via an interactive whiteboard, asks questions about the material presented, and directs students to copy particular notes.

In another classroom across the hall, Ms. Searson introduces an English language arts lesson by explaining the step-by-step instructions students will need to follow in order to accomplish the objectives of the lesson. The students, many of whom are English language learners (ELLs), switch from Spanish to English as they exchange ideas with one another briefly before the task begins.

Although Ms. Searson's students are initially seated in rows, the movable desks are easily brought together, and her students are invited to collaborate in pairs or trios. The students work in tandem; yet other than the permitted use of students' native language, there is little adaptation, forethought, or organization for small-group instruction to address the students' needs.

At the same school, Mr. Banner, a science teacher, is preparing to introduce his biology lesson to a class of eighth graders. Students enter and congregate around the room, freely conversing in Spanish and in English in

127

spite of the period bell that has just signaled the class to begin. Mr. Banner makes multiple attempts to redirect his students to their seats where they finally settle down to focus on the initial activity projected on the board. Students' attention during the lesson varies, and there are a great many conversations occurring throughout the lesson between students that have nothing to do with what is being taught.

THE CHALLENGE OF MIDDLE SCHOOLS

American middle schools, serving as the halfway point between elementary school and high school, have their own unique challenges as they represent a critical time in the lives of young adolescent students. Current attention to higher standards and increased accountability through academic testing has created undue pressure on middle-school communities.

When youngsters transition to middle school, they face a new system of regulations, responsibilities, routines, and available support (Maton, Schellenbach, Leadbeater, & Solarz, 2004), often leading to an increase in their anxiety and stress, which ultimately impacts school behavior. Considerable biological and cognitive changes occur in middle-school adolescents. They often are more self-conscious and may lack self-esteem, and yet they begin to understand more complex concepts as well as think more abstractly.

Middle-school students also strive for autonomy and independence and have a strong desire to make their own decisions as they also become more peer oriented (Maton et al., 2004). Still, these youngsters often lack a certain level of maturity as evidenced frequently by their inappropriate classroom behavior. For this reason, middle-school teachers often enforce stricter control and discipline and allow less autonomy with this student population as illustrated in the chapter opening vignettes (Eccles et al., 1993; Emmer & Evertson, 2012; Ridnour, 2006).

With the adoption of the Common Core State Standards (CCSS), National Governors Association Center for Best Practices (NGA)/Council of Chief State School Officers (CCSSO) (2010), and more particularly, the speaking and listening strand of the English language arts standards, students will need to collaborate with one another during class time to meet clear learning objectives.

The CCSS document contains a note on the range and content of student speaking and listening in that "students must have ample opportunities to take part in a variety of rich, structured conversations—as part of a whole class, in small groups, and with a partner—built around important content" (NGA/CCSSO, 2010, p. 48). With these expectations, developing a new set of classroom management strategies is most crucial for all secondary teachers.

THREE TEACHERS—THREE DIFFERENT CLASSROOM MANAGEMENT STYLES

Strong teacher-student relationships are central to ensuring student success. For Wolk (2003), "classroom management is not separate from teaching and not something that a teacher must achieve before teaching can begin. […] The best discipline and curriculum are, in turn, built on caring and trusting relationships" (para. 8–9). If the goal is to increase student collaboration and in the process not surrender student discipline, it is important to establish relationships in the classroom that foster trust, respect, and caring.

The three teachers described at the beginning of the chapter have different teaching styles, levels of tolerance, and classroom management skills that contribute to the types of teacher-student relationships that exist. We examine their approaches to teaching and learning in order to discern how their present practices may facilitate or impede effective, collaborative student discussions as outlined by the CCSS.

Teacher-Centered Interaction

Ms. Malone employs a *teacher-centered interaction* approach that is characterized by desks arranged in rows, a traditional question-answer format, and individual student work. Student-to-student and teacher-to-student interactions are controlled, and students speak only when asked by the teacher to respond to questions.

In classrooms where teachers are reluctant to release control, there are few opportunities for students to shape the curriculum and create a shared community of learning. Interaction occurs in a one-way direction, from the teacher toward the students or the students toward the teacher.

The teacher controls what content and topics are taught as well as how they are assessed and uses a direct or lecture-style method of instruction to maintain management. Students learn that the only audience they need to address and please is the sole authority in the room, the source of all information, the teacher. Individual work prevails, and student input is limited to responses to teacher-posed questions.

Undifferentiated Student-Centered Interaction

Ms. Searson provides opportunities for *student-centered interaction* in her class. Her management of the class seems more fluid, yet remains structured as evidenced by her students being engaged in conversations that pertain to the lesson. However, the collaboration is not scaffolded in that there is limited use of strategies and activities that would benefit the diverse students in her class.

The teacher releases control to students when she puts them in groups because she knows that cooperative tasks are beneficial to them, but she does not address the particular needs of her academically and linguistically diverse students. Students who would benefit from additional support are randomly grouped and complete the same assigned tasks as their more capable peers with few, if any, adaptations.

Unfocused Student-Centered Interaction

Mr. Banner's instruction is the least structured of the three teaching styles, and even though collaboration occurs, it is usually nondirected and unfocused. One may perceive the classroom as chaotic—but even in many classrooms where some level of disorder ensues, learning takes place. Rather, Mr. Banner's class for the most part remains unstructured and lacks opportunities for purposeful and meaningful interaction. Students seem to have all the control, and the teacher is often unable to direct students to remain on task.

The challenge to consider is how to best help these teachers to develop instructional practices in combination with classroom management skills in order to best facilitate the CCSS framework for speaking and listening. In what ways can these three teachers increase student collaboration yet maintain their individual teaching styles and comfort levels?

RESHAPING CLASSROOM PRACTICES

According to Marzano (2003), the most effective teacher-student relationships are characterized by specific teacher behaviors: exhibiting appropriate levels of dominance, maintaining balanced cooperation, and being aware of high-needs students" (p. 8). These intended behaviors are for the most part the key to classroom management success.

Additionally, in order for students to remain on task, teachers must give thoughtful attention to their individual needs, which may include addressing different learning styles, strengths, preferences, abilities, and readiness levels through techniques that foster learning for all. Yet, concentrating on the needs of individual learners will not suffice when it comes to meeting a set of rigorous listening and speaking standards.

With the changing expectations as presented by the CCSS, teachers must now develop ways in which students can actively engage in a range of collaborative conversations in class. Students must be able to not only listen to another student's point of view but also evaluate sound reasoning and substantive evidence for that student's particular claims.

To conduct such conversations, students will require a broad set of new skills that include focused attention to and examination of information details concerning academic content. To facilitate these skills, some teachers will have to minimize their teacher-centered interactions while others may have to find more meaningful ways for students to conduct discourse while maintaining control.

Directed Group Work

In most middle schools, traditional direct instruction takes place with the exception of some classes that employ group work. In the least effective use of group work, students are randomly grouped and asked to complete a task with little, if any, delineation of objectives, explicit instruction, teacher guidance, or progress monitoring.

The best or most studious group member, more often than not, reluctantly completes all of the work and hands it in to the teacher for credit that will apply to the entire group. Sometimes teachers assign individual grades as well as group grades to counter inequities often associated with group work. However, this has not proven to be a panacea for the hardworking individual students who shoulder the majority of the assignment.

Quinn (2013) argued that "group work is neither as widely used nor as effective as necessary if we wish to produce a generation of learners adept at collaborating. In fact, group work as often practiced does little to enhance collaborative skills" (p. 47). Yet, group work allows students to:

- take part in rich conversations, one on one or in groups, with diverse partners that build on others' ideas,
- acquire new content knowledge,
- build communication and collaboration skills,
- enhance their self-esteem,
- apply critical thinking skills, and
- develop positive relations with teacher and peers.

The Rules of Engagement

In order for students to participate successfully in collaborative conversations, they must be mindful of the rules for cooperative discourse, establish needed conversational roles, and focus on objectives as well as the time limitations of specific tasks (NGA/CCSSO, 2010). For example, seventh-grade students must be able to "follow rules for collegial discussions, track progress toward specific goals and deadlines, and define individual roles as needed" (NGA/CCSSO, 2010, p. 49).

They must be directed toward developing a set of guidelines for civil discourse: engaging in active listening, focusing on evidence and facts, using reason and collaborative problem solving, and avoiding personal attacks (Mars, 2011). Students must take part in the decision making for their roles and responsibilities in organized conversations and come to consensus about how they will conduct themselves in conversational activities.

In this way, students will have ownership of the behaviors they exhibit, and with ample practice, be able to self-monitor their adherence to the agreed-upon guidelines. In addition, ongoing assessment of how students converse collaboratively must be in place in order to maintain a positive learning environment as well as offer students feedback about meeting agreed-upon expectations.

PROFESSIONAL LEARNING COMMUNITIES

One way for teachers to develop the needed skills to manage their classrooms is to participate in a *professional learning community* (PLC) (DuFour, 2004; DuFour & Eaker, 1998). According to Roberts and Pruitt (2009), a learning community "provides a vehicle for teachers to share ideas about standards-based instruction" (p. 12). This type of professional learning for teachers often translates into improved student outcomes.

In the case of the three teachers described in this chapter, establishing a PLC that fosters active collaboration, reflection, and honest dialogue about classroom practices between and among those who share the same pupils or similar challenges would bring about needed change. By each teacher capitalizing on his or her strengths and creatively problem solving together, their shared ideas can help build particular learning environments for their students who, in turn, can also be guided to engage in collaborative conversations themselves.

As one possible scenario for our featured teachers working in a PLC, Ms. Malone might describe how she is able to maintain control of her students, Ms. Searson might identify her management of student group work, and Mr. Banner might share how he developed his high-level of tolerance for elevated classroom sound and student activity. Together, they focus on how to better structure their class lessons to increase effective conversational practices for their students and how to train them in the rules of engagement. As each of them incorporates new ideas for managing their classes, they can return to the group for further support, guidance, and encouragement.

RECOMMENDATIONS TO INCREASE STUDENT COLLABORATION

Successful classroom management for effective student-to-student collaboration requires some critical approaches—ground rules, adequate class time, and established routines—to engage students in focused learning, increase their use of academic language in conversation, and make class sessions more meaningful. In addition, the forum for teachers to safely explore and discuss procedures for how to begin and maintain student collaboration; how to share successful routines, false starts, and the challenges of managing student groups; and how to take risks as well as engage in reflective practices can be accomplished through PLCs.

As general guidelines for classroom practices to promote effective student collaboration, teachers should develop class routines to explain the purpose of tasks, offer clear and precise directions that ensure students understand what they need to do, discuss the scope and time limit of student discussions, and articulate their expectations. Teachers will also need to make the rules for collaboration explicit. Students need to follow rules for collegial discussions and decision making, pose questions, respond to others' questions and comments, acknowledge new information, and justify their own ideas.

Working in PLCs, teachers can further explore how to purposefully group students according to various levels of readiness, levels of interest, preferences, and academic and communication skills or when to allow students the choice of groups. Furthermore, PLCs may also provide the framework for teachers to discuss how best to monitor and guide student interactions, how to redirect off-task conversations, or how to adjust student assignments so that all students remain engaged in meeting the Common Core speaking and listening standards.

REFERENCES

DuFour, R. (2004). What is a professional learning community? *Educational Leadership, 61*(8), 6–11.

DuFour, R., & Eaker, R. (1998). *Professional learning communities at work: Best practices for enhancing student achievement.* Bloomington, IN: Solution Tree.

Eccles, J. S., Midgley, C., Wigfield, A., Buchanan, C. M., Reuman, D., Flanagan, C., et al. (1993). Development during adolescence: The impact of stage-environment fit on young adolescents' experiences in schools and families. *American Psychologist, 48*, 90–101.

Emmer, E. T., & Evertson, C. M. (2012). *Classroom management for middle and high school teachers* (9th ed.). Boston, MA: Pearson.

Mars, R. (2011). *Seven rules for civil discourse.* Retrieved from http://open.salon.com/blog/robmars/2011/01/20/seven_rules_for_civil_discourse

Marzano, R. J. (2003).*What works in schools.* Alexandria, VA: ASCD.

Maton, K. I., Schellenbach, B. J., Leadbeater, B. J., & Solarz, A. L. (Eds.) (2004). *Investing in children, youth, and families: Strength-based research and policy.* Washington, DC: American Psychological Association.

National Governors Association Center for Best Practices and Council of Chief State School Officers, (2010). *Common Core State Standards for English language arts and literacy in history/social studies, science, and technical subjects.* Retrieved from http://www .corestandards.org/assets/CCSSI_ELA%20Standards.pdf.

Quinn, T. (2013). G-r-o-u-p-w-o-r-k doesn't spell collaboration. *Phi Delta Kappan, 94*(4), 46–48.

Ridnour, K. (2006). *Managing your classroom with heart: A guide for nurturing adolescent learners.* Alexandria, VA: ASCD.

Roberts, S. M., & Pruitt, E. Z. (2009). *Schools as professional learning communities: Collaborative activities and strategies for professional development*. Thousand Oaks, CA: Corwin Press.

Wolk, S. (2003). Hearts and minds. *Educational Leadership, 61*(1), 14-18.

Chapter Seventeen

Defusing Conflict in the Classroom with Restorative Practices

Luanna H. Meyer and Ian M. Evans

Samuel is 12 years old and has just started middle school. In contrast to elementary school, where he spent the day with one teacher, he goes from room to room for classes taught by different subject teachers. It is early in the school year, so it is an adjustment for both the students and teachers who do not know each other well. For some students, records have not yet arrived from the district office about their individual learning or behavior challenges.

Samuel's math teacher, Mr. Maxwell, realizes that he has several students who seem to be struggling academically and who may have been referred to intervention services in the past for behavior problems. Samuel seems to be one of those students and Mr. Maxwell has heard a couple of stories about him from other teachers.

The math class is large, and the workload is substantial. Nevertheless, Mr. Maxwell thinks it is important to develop a rapport with his students and to know about their learning style and find out about them personally. One of his strategies is the practice of having individual students bring a piece of work to his desk to discuss privately, away from the rest of the group; there is a chair permanently located by the side of the teacher's desk for this purpose. He is able to have these one-on-one conversations with students during class time whenever they are working independently or in groups.

To ensure that calling students up for these individual talks is not stigmatizing, he tries to avoid any pattern of approaching only high or low achievers. After two weeks, the students seem comfortable with this routine, and he hopes to have individual time with everyone by the end of the month. Mr. Maxwell's longer term plan is for this practice to provide a normalized context for addressing behavioral challenges as well as academic work.

Twice a week, Mr. Maxwell starts class with a 10-minute period to check assigned homework, and he reviews work informally as he walks from desk to desk. This is one of those days, and the students are working quietly. Suddenly, Samuel shouts, "What are you laughing at, you f*@#ers?!" Mr. Maxwell looks across the room towards Samuel and says firmly, "Samuel, quiet!" Samuel growls and looks down at his desk. He does not seem to have a pen so he walks to the front of the room where there are extra pens for student use during class.

The incident is not over. Mr. Maxwell has been moving closer to where Samuel is sitting and is now watching Samuel out of the corner of his eye. This time he sees what happens as Samuel walks by other students and taps their desks with the tip of his pen. One of the students mumbles "Stop that, you jerk!" in a low voice. Samuel replies loudly, "Why should I, loser?!" Mr. Maxwell is closer now and says, "Samuel, I'll be there in a minute to see what's happening." Rather than returning to his seat, Samuel stands where he is, looks defiant and blurts out, "So what—I don't care what you do!"

Mr. Maxwell is generally liked by the students and known for having a safe classroom environment that supports teaching and learning. He is committed to constructive approaches to challenging behavior, having attended recent workshops on restorative practices and positive behavior support (PBS). But in this instance, there has been an altercation in class between students, and Samuel has verbally confronted the teacher in full view of the entire class.

Now what? He could send Samuel to the office as a consequence for disobedience and verbally confronting the teacher. This would be considered punishment, on the assumption that Samuel does not want to go to the office, hence he would not repeat abusive comments to other students and to the teacher in the future. The teacher, however, does not want to escalate the problem, and he thinks it would be impossible for Samuel to save face and deal constructively with similar challenges in the future if this turns into a formal discipline event. It might not be too late to salvage the situation and also use it to build better relationships with Samuel and his classmates at the same time.

And there is more: What if Samuel's disruptiveness was motivated by not having done the homework because he did not understand or have the skills to complete the worksheets? The teacher also does not know for sure that Samuel started it; it is possible that taunts from other students provoked the incident. If Samuel ends up feeling wronged by seeing someone else get away with being mean to him, he would come away from the experience feeling even more hostile than he does now.

Mr. Maxwell knows that anything to get out of the classroom could be a reward, according to applied behavior analysis principles (Evans, 2001). Being sent to the office could be *reinforcement* for Samuel's challenging behavior by allowing him to escape something aversive—the math homework. He would be able to leave the classroom without revealing that he cannot do the work.

Sending Samuel to the office also provides a reinforcing situation to other students (including the one who challenged Samuel) and even the teacher, since with Samuel removed, the class could get back to their work without perceived interruptions and distractions. Mr. Maxwell knows what he will do. But before describing what happens next, some background information on restorative practices will be helpful.

PRINCIPLES AND PRACTICES OF RESTORATIVE CLASSROOM DISCIPLINE

Mr. Maxwell's teaching reflects the principles and practices of restorative classroom discipline (Meyer & Evans, 2012a). The basic premise of restorative discipline practices is that students are more likely to be cooperative, feel respected, and make positive changes when those in authority do things with them, rather than to them.

Ideally, the entire school would be committed to the broad framework of restorative school discipline (Meyer & Evans, 2012b), but individual teachers can adopt key elements of restorative classroom discipline as outlined in Table 17.1 even in schools with more traditional disciplinary procedures.

Since several teachers were trying some of the approaches, the principal and her team could monitor results compared with typical practices. They were committed to using evidence to evaluate whether restorative practices would be effective in their large, urban middle school, where there were minor discipline events but also difficult challenges (for more information on user-friendly data collection, see Meyer & Evans, 2012a).

Restorative Classroom Conferences

The teachers in Mr. Maxwell's group have agreed that their intervention will start with *restorative classroom conferences* to engage students in problem solving—emphasizing restoration and restitution rather than punishment and retribution. When an incident occurs, the teacher talks to students individually using a *generative restorative script* to allow students to tell their side of the story and to be heard—ending with reflections about the overall situation and discussion of possible solutions (Drewery, 2004).

When Mr. Maxwell talks privately with Samuel or another student at his desk during class, these brief conversations address the present problem and help to build positive relationships with students. After hearing from Samuel, the teacher would next interview other students, privately and individually, who were involved in the incident.

Key Element	Definition
Restorative Principles and Practices	Underlying valuing of inclusion and relationships, addressing behavioral challenges through restoration of relationships and making amends for wrongdoing.
Classroom Ethos and Climate	Each member of the classroom community feels valued and takes responsibility for the well-being of others.
Culturally Responsive Pedagogies	Cultural and linguistic diversity viewed as strengths, deficit explanations for failure based on differences rejected, and teaching responsive to cultural differences.
Restorative Discipline	Interpretation of conflict and behavioral incidents as breakdowns in positive relationships requiring restitution and restoration follow-up, not blame, punishment, or exclusion.
Teacher Agency	Agentic teachers who take responsibility for all students' learning and well-being, excluding no one.
Inclusive	Strong sense of safety, mutual respect, and belonging for all students, without exclusion consequences for conflict and challenges.
Behavioral Expectations	Agreed expectations for behavior and social-emotional understandings within the classroom and school, constructed with input from students, family, and the community.
Problem Solving	Informal and formal processes, including restorative classroom conferencing, used to address conflict and disruptions in the classroom.
Peer Support	Ongoing informal and formal cooperative peer networks, group work, and mediation in the classroom for behavioral and learning issues.
Restorative Curricula	Support for developmentally and age-appropriate expectations for restorative interpersonal behavior and understandings through everyday classroom conversations and conflict prevention and resolution.
Home-School Connections	Ongoing positive relationships with children's families for meaningful family input and engagement in children's learning and behavior.

Table 17.1

Key Elements of Restorative Classroom Discipline

The generative restorative script follows this sequence of questions:

- *What happened?*
- *What do you think about what happened?*
- *What might someone else think about what happened?*
- *Who has been affected by what happened?*
- *In what way?*
- *What do you think has to happen next to make things better?*

As teachers become more experienced in using the script, they develop the flexibility to vary these questions for particular events, circumstances, language, and culture.

While using this semi-formal script, teachers engage in active, nonjudgmental listening and model those skills for children. Students with behavioral challenges are often not accustomed to having someone listen to their version of events, and teachers need to work hard to listen carefully and not interrupt, even if what the child is saying seems completely wrong. The student may need to get something off his or her chest and, once heard, will be more amenable to moving forward to explore solutions. This is true for any child, not just those with behavioral challenges.

Adults may be in the habit of leaping to interpretations that fit preconceived ideas about people and events, failing to hear others out and listen to information that gives a much clearer and more accurate picture of what happened. Listening carefully to another person—both other professionals and children—communicates fundamental respect, just as failing to hear the other side of the story shuts people down and may communicate a righteous-sounding assertion of a power imbalance. Listening carefully will also help understand the child's thought processes, which can be distorted and which is something adults need to know.

Restorative Small Group Conferences

The teacher uses the same approach of restorative conferencing for problem-solving incidents or challenges in small group discussions of five to six students at a time:

- *Can someone tell me what happened?*
- *Can I tell you what happened from my perspective? Does anyone else see it differently?*
- *How do you feel about that?*
- *Could you each tell me how you see things? Let's have _____ go first and after she has finished, _____ can give his perspective. After both of you have explained what happened, then we can try to sort this out.*

In these conversations, the teacher is neutral and focuses on supporting students to identify what needs to be done to either make amends or move on if the problem cannot be solved right away. School personnel should be prepared to use this nonconfrontational conversation in multiple contexts—for example, in the school lunchroom or on the playground when a negative interaction between students has happened.

When he conducts classroom conferences, Mr. Maxwell keeps in mind that students have varying levels of social-emotional development at different ages. Thus, during these restorative conferences, he expects that students will show different capacities to understand social interactions. Teachers can benefit from understanding the general chronological changes highlighted by Cavanagh (2007) as follows:

- *Ages 5–6*: Children know that everyone has feelings and that individuals can respond in various ways—feelings may not be the same. They begin to develop empathy by seeing how another child feels about something. Children begin to learn what a friendship is, as opposed to simply playing together.
- *Ages 7–9*: Children understand the dynamics of friendships and belonging to a group. They can learn to listen, trust, speak honestly from the heart, and be respectful of others. They should start to learn negotiation and mediation skills, rather than insisting on their own perspectives or desires at the expense of others.
- *Ages 10–11*: In addition to all the above, children can speak truthfully and with respect—they can be diplomatic. They can develop peacemaking skills and be part of group problem solving (e.g., through conferencing).
- *Ages 12–17*: Teenagers can engage in restorative conversations that do not confuse the problem with the person. They can embrace major responsibilities for problem-solving group conferences, either formally in classrooms or informally with peers and friends.

Through his restorative classroom conferences, Mr. Maxwell is supporting the development of these age-appropriate socio-emotional understandings.

Applying Restorative Classroom Discipline

Mr. Maxwell knows that the first step is to defuse the incident involving Samuel without allowing more social-emotional harm to be done, such as festering conflict and interpersonal resentments. Trying to preserve everyone's dignity, he moves toward Samuel and asks firmly but calmly, "Samuel, would you sit down now please?" Samuel looks glum—even angry—but he does what the teacher asks.

Telling the class to "Please keep working, you have five more minutes to finish," Mr. Maxwell sees that Samuel's worksheets are blank. He asks Samuel to complete the first problem, but Samuel glowers at the page and does not respond. Mr. Maxwell then tells him to come up to his desk at the front to get another page: Samuel complies, and they walk together to the teacher's desk where Samuel takes his seat in the extra chair.

Mr. Maxwell suspects that the work might be too hard for Samuel, so he needs more information about his math skills. For now, he asks for Samuel's side of the story about the altercation, with the first restorative conferencing question: *What happened?* Samuel responds with anger directed to another student who, he says, always picks on him. He argues that the teachers never see what the other students do, but just blame everything on him. Mr. Maxwell listens quietly to Samuel's answers.

Samuel is not happy, but he participates and seems to calm down. His answers do not show a great deal of empathy, but he seems positive about Mr. Maxwell's plans to talk with the other student he has accused and for them to talk again about what to do in the future.

Mr. Maxwell gives Samuel a new worksheet targeted at a lower level, asking him to finish it by the start of class tomorrow. This will allow the teacher to learn more about Samuel's math skills and capabilities. He also needs to find out how other students might be contributing to Samuel's problems, and then he'll be in a better position to take action. Thus, once Samuel returns to his seat, Mr. Maxwell repeats the process with the other student who was named.

This restorative conferencing approach is designed to establish mutual respect, support clear expectations for class behavior, and strengthen trusting relationships with the students.

SUMMARY

Restorative classroom discipline is not a single strategy or formula. Rather, it reflects commitment to restorative practices with the primary purpose of developing positive relationships and supporting the peaceful resolution of conflict by teachers and students. Nor is it a behavior management system, though it encompasses the essential elements of positive behavior management that have been characterized as *educative* (Evans & Meyer, 1985), *nonaversive* (Meyer & Evans, 1989), or *positive behavior support* (Dunlap, Sailor, Horner, & Sugai, 2009).

Restorative classroom discipline has strong empirical support for intervening with individual children's behavior challenges in typical schools (McCluskey et al., 2008). It differs from behavior management approaches in its overarching focus on relationships alongside organizational and cultural contexts.

The approach is not bottom-up in emphasizing descriptions of acceptable and unacceptable behavior within deficit-intervention frameworks. Nor is it top-down in asserting classroom rules set by the teacher, whereby incidents are viewed as transgressions against rules. Instead, restorative classroom discipline is people focused, accepting that positive and supportive relationships are crucial for learning to occur in educational environments. Conflict must be addressed by making amends and restitution so that relationships are not damaged or even broken.

Restorative classroom discipline also goes beyond being simply a philosophy or set of principles. Restorative classroom discipline concurs with the societal goal that the primary purpose of schools is to *educate*. This responsibility to educate involves more than a focus on basic skills such as literacy, numeracy, and subject knowledge: it includes education for citizenship and becoming contributing members of one's community.

Thus, restorative practices are grounded in educative principles for providing all members of the school community with skills and understandings about positive social interactions and relationships that support learning and peaceful resolution of problems and conflict.

REFERENCES

Cavanagh, T. (2007). Focusing on relationships creates safety in schools. *Set: Research Information for Teachers, 1,* 31–35.

Drewery, W. (2004). Conferencing in schools: Punishment, restorative justice, and the productive importance of the process of conversation. *Journal of Community and Applied Social Psychology, 14,* 332–344.

Dunlap, G., Sailor, W., Horner, R. H., & Sugai, G. (2009). Overview and history of positive behavior support. In W. Sailor, G. Dunlap, G. Sugai, & R. Horner (Eds.), *Handbook of positive behavior support* (pp. 3–16). New York, NY: Springer.

Evans, I. M. (2001). Reinforcement, principle of. In N. J. Smelser & P. B. Baltes (Eds. in Chief), *International encyclopedia of the social and behavioral sciences: Clinical and applied psychology* (pp. 400–410). Oxford, UK: Elsevier Science.

Evans, I. M., & Meyer, L. H. (1985). *An educative approach to behavior problems: A practical decision model for interventions with severely handicapped learners.* Baltimore, MD: Paul H. Brookes.

McCluskey, G., Lloyd, G., Kane, J., Riddell, S., Stead, J., & Weedon, E. (2008). Can restorative practices in schools make a difference? *Educational Review, 60,* 405–417.

Meyer, L. H., & Evans, I. M. (1989). *Nonaversive intervention for behavior problems: A manual for home and community.* Baltimore, MD: Paul H. Brookes.

Meyer, L. H., & Evans, I. M. (2012a). *The teacher's guide to restorative classroom discipline.* Thousand Oaks, CA: Corwin Press.

Meyer, L. H., & Evans, I. M. (2012b). *The school leader's guide to restorative school discipline.* Thousand Oaks, CA: Corwin Press.

Chapter Eighteen

Managing Math and Supervising Spanish: Establishing and Maintaining Positive Classroom Culture in the Middle School

Martha Edelson and Lori Langer de Ramirez

As teachers of middle school math and world language, we do not like the term *classroom management*. The concepts of *management* and *supervision* are inapposite in the context of our classes. We do not feel as if we *manage* our adolescent students; rather, we strive to expose them to a rich and exciting curriculum, foster trusting relationships, and provide classroom behavior parameters in which everyone can feel safe, secure, and happy.

There are many effective ways that we have found to work with our *tween* students that foster greater self-monitoring and positive peer pressure as a means of establishing a positive—and productive—classroom environment in middle school math and Spanish.

BODY LANGUAGE

Students in our classes are keenly aware of their teachers' every move, gesture, and mannerism. They even notice when we wear a new article of clothing or if we have changed our hairstyle. So it is natural that they often seem to respond as much to our body language and facial expressions as they do to our words. As detailed below, we have found ways to leverage this attention to visual, spatial, and auditory cues as a means of conveying expectations to students in our classes.

Pauses and Proxemics

One technique that we use in the immersion-style language classroom is called *Motherese*. Essentially, it is meant to mimic the way a mother (or father) might speak incessantly to babies, despite the fact that the child does not yet understand the words. The idea is that children learn languages by being exposed to examples of speech in many different situations, over and over again. In the world language classroom, this strategy involves teachers using the target language to expose students to examples of contextualized speech throughout the lesson.

For example, as students walk into the classroom, the teacher might greet them in the following ways: "¿Qué hay, Lauren? Me encantan tus zapatos. ¡Hola, Zach! ¿Qué tal te fue anoche con el partido? ¿Ganaron? (What's up, Lauren. I love your shoes. Hi, Zach! How did it go with the game last night? Did you win?)" Students may not understand the teacher completely (some say that they do not understand a thing!), but most comprehend some words, chunks of language, and phrases.

Motherese also sets up a norm of classroom discourse that involves a certain frenetic energy. This can be used to the teacher's advantage when needing to call students to attention. When students must pay special attention, or the teacher wants to convey dissatisfaction with certain student behaviors, it is effective to simply shut up.

Students are not used to their Spanish teacher being silent for very long, and they very quickly calm down and look at the teacher for direction. The silence can start with a student or two, and then will spread through the classroom like a wave. Once the teacher has everyone's attention, the point can be made. By interrupting the normal state of the class, the teacher can quickly and easily get students to focus.

Another technique that works in the language classroom involves proxemics—a form of nonverbal communication that involves the use of space and distances. As students work in pairs or teams on activities in class, the teacher walks around the room to check on their progress and help students who might be struggling. Since one of the key elements of the immersion classroom is almost exclusive use of the target language, it is essential that the teacher circulate to keep students *in the language*. The teacher's physical proximity also serves as a reminder to speak only in Spanish, as this is often one of the agreed-upon classroom rules.

During lessons, teachers can also use proximity to students as a means of conveying dissatisfaction with negative student behaviors. For example, if the teacher notices that a student is texting or doing science homework (the horror!), by simply walking over to the student's desk the teacher can correct the behavior. Alternatively, gingerly leaning on the desk with fingers or hand indicates that the teacher is paying attention to the student and the inappropriate behavior.

Just One of the Gang

In a subject as fraught with a range of emotional responses as math, it is especially important that teachers relay both a sense of enthusiasm and understanding with their bodies. To foster a sense of community and to allow students to feel control over their behavior and learning, a teacher can "join the group." She sits with the students as another student demonstrates a problem-solving strategy on the board. Moving about as they work, giving a reassuring smile or laughing with a student, and sitting among them as the class has discussions, a teacher is rarely in front of the class.

In addition to heeding body language, a teacher can pay close attention to the way she uses her voice. For example, a teacher once came to school with laryngitis. She could not speak and she noticed that her students were all whispering as though they could not speak either. She now rarely raises her voice and never raises it above theirs. She has learned that when a teacher raises her voice the class becomes louder.

When a teacher wants to gain the class's attention, it is helpful to speak softly or even to whisper. Those who notice quickly hush other students and soon the whole class is attentive. This technique is particularly difficult for some with effusive personalities, and one needs to be conscious of the tone that one sets in the classroom. As soon as a teacher becomes too loud, the students often do as well.

ESTABLISHING CLASSROOM NORMS

Experience has taught us that students choose to behave the way they do and, as Anderson (2003) asserted in *Cooperative Discipline*, they are propelled by a desire to belong. Thus, it is important for teachers to work with students to create a code of conduct that works for all and that engenders a positive classroom community. The goal for this code is to create norms whereby everyone contributes to a constructive learning environment.

Asking students to envision the ideal classroom allows them to take responsibility for their own and their peers' conduct. Furthermore, students can be asked to identify specific behaviors that exemplify each broader mode of conduct. Anderson (2003) also suggested that, when students participate in developing a set of consequences, they are more likely to consider them reasonable. Posting the code on the wall and referring to it frequently enables students to internalize positive behaviors.

El Contrato—A Class Contract

The first day of Spanish class could involve a thoughtful and open discussion about how one learns languages and the kind of classroom community that would best facilitate learning. Using a class wiki space, students are asked to brainstorm a list of things that they should do in class to maximize their chances of success during the year. Using this asynchronous web-based tool allows students to add, delete, and edit their class list from home. As it is a democratic space, with all users having equal power over the content, it establishes a sense of cooperation and collaboration right from the start. Students come up with an impressive list every year. Among the perennial comments are:

- Don't talk when people are talking.
- Don't forget to bring books to class.
- Don't speak English.
- Don't make fun of classmates when they don't remember a word.
- Don't do other work when you should be doing Spanish.
- Don't be disrespectful of classmates or the teacher.
- Don't call out.

Since much of students' experience with discipline in school might be characterized as negative reinforcement (i.e., "Don't run in the halls."), the class continues to edit the wiki to rephrase the admonitions as positive statements:

- Listen quietly when people are talking.
- Remember to bring books to class.
- Speak Spanish.
- Help classmates when they don't remember a word.
- Do your Spanish work in class.
- Be respectful of classmates and the teacher.
- Raise your hand and wait to be called on to participate.

With this student-generated list of desired classroom behaviors, a student contract is developed and shared with parents online. A poster-sized version of the class rules is also posted in the classroom. When a student breaks the rules in class, *classmates* often point to the poster and read the line that corresponds to the particular infraction.

    Establishing student-developed and agreed-upon rules at the beginning of the year helps to create community and set up expectations right from the start. Using the web-based wiki space adds to the collaborative nature of the activity and provides a public space along with a larger shared audience for the rules.

Turn-taking in Math

In a math class, it is common for some children—often boys—to dominate the conversation. These children perform calculations quickly and tend to be confident in their skills. Their boisterous participation, while fueled by enthusiasm and good intentions, can shut down others. It is at these times that a teacher can circle back to the class code and remind students that all children have an equal right to learn. Allowing those highly expressive students outlets for their enjoyment, though, is essential.

A teacher can have students write down what they want to say and assure them that they will have a chance to share their problem-solving strategies with the class once everyone has had a chance to work on the math problem. Those who work quickly can also check their work with one another. In addition, there are always optional challenge problems to work on when students have completed the regular assignment. Assuring that all have an opportunity to participate also ensures that those who need more time are provided with it.

GROUP WORK AND POSITIVE PEER PRESSURE

When a group is asked to perform a specific assignment or task, it is important to make expectations explicit—especially with tweens and teens. How will the groups work together? What is important for each member to do to be a successful group member? How can conflicts be resolved? Having discussions with the students about expectations before commencing a group project can go a long way in preventing difficulties and assuring a successful outcome for each group. When the teacher provides a tight structure for group work, the students feel safe working with each other.

Discipline with a Smile

In the Spanish classroom, it is imperative that students work together to understand classroom directions given in Spanish and maintain their own use of Spanish during interactive tasks. In order to facilitate group work and interpersonal communication, students are seated in pods (groups of four desks facing each other). At the start of each class, two laminated "smiley/ sad faces" (the ubiquitous emoticon printed on laminated yellow paper) are distributed to each pod.

Each smiley face represents a point for the pod, so the assumption is that each pod earns two points just for showing up to class! As class progresses each day, student behavior is monitored using these faces. If a student is misbehaving (i.e., off-task, using English rather than Spanish during an activity), the smiley face is turned over to reveal a sad face on the reverse side.

This indicates a warning to students; if the students exhibit improved behavior, the face is turned back to the smiley side—no harm, no foul.

If negative behavior continues after the sad face is revealed, it is possible to lose the face entirely, leaving only one face (one point) on the desk. When a pod reaches a certain number of points, the members receive a reward.

The smiley face point system works well for several reasons. It assumes good behavior by rewarding points up front. Students get the message that they are expected to be well-behaved, engaged, and respectful members of the classroom community. Since there are intermediary steps in place before a face is taken away from a group, students are given the chance to change their behavior before permanent harm is done.

Classmates take on the role of policing the group and are inevitably more effective and perceived as less intimidating than the teacher. Having a student whisper "Shhh!" to a classmate sitting nearby also allows the offender to save face more easily than if the teacher would have to stop class to correct the student more publicly. Finally, this system encourages teamwork and fosters community as the pod team works together to gain points and be the first to reap the rewards after 50 points are gathered.

Specific Roles and Self-evaluation in Math Groups

One strategy that helps facilitate effective group work is to assign individual group member roles, such as facilitator or note taker, which rotate daily or weekly. Each role is clearly defined, with written guidelines that delineate the expectations. Rotating roles ensures that each student has various opportunities to participate effectively.

Empowering students to become responsible for their own behavior and for each other is the most effective way of managing group work. In *Literature Circles*, Daniels (2002) suggested that using a *process checker* sheet is a powerful tool to help students in this endeavor. These checklists are adaptable to group processes in any subject and lend themselves effectively to group problem solving in math. Also, to allow students to reflect on their performance, it is best to stop the activity several minutes before the end of class.

The teacher then distributes the *Individual Checklist* (Figure 18.1) for each student to reflect on his or her participation privately. Next, the teacher distributes the *Group Checklist* (Figure 18.2) so that the students in each group can discuss their performance that day and set goals for a subsequent session. Allowing students this time to reflect makes it possible for them to manage their own participation in group work.

Name _____

Job _____

Group Problem Solving
How Did I Do?

✔ + : above and beyond

✔ : did job, prepared, stayed focused during discussion, participated in discussion

✔ - : minimal effort on HW, did not do job well, did not stay focused during discussion, minimal participation

_____ _____ _____
How well you did   Participation   Focus
your job

Comments:

Figure 18.1.   Individual Checklist

Name _____

Job _____

Group Problem Solving
How Did WE Do?

✔ + : above and beyond

✔ : Pretty good all around

✔ - : Struggled

_____ _____ _____
How well each person   Everyone Participated   Everyone was Focused
did job

What we did well today:

Our goal as a group for next time:

Figure 18.2.   Group Checklist

CONCLUSION

Classroom management in the middle school can often feel like herding cats, but there are rewards for working with this age group. Adolescent students are quixotic; one day calm and centered, the next day frantic and overemotional. In order to best work with tweens, we have found that it is important to have clearly defined norms and goals, an opportunity for self-reflection for students, and the possibility for students to exert at least some control over their classroom environment. For the teacher of adolescents, it is beneficial to have a positive outlook, to be flexible, and to be extremely patient. It also helps to love these kids—including their quirks and instabilities—and to have an excellent sense of humor!

In their book *Handbook of Classroom Management*, Evertson and Weinstein (2006) defined classroom management as "the actions teachers take to create an environment that supports and facilitates both academic and social-emotional learning" (p. 4).

The techniques we have shared here fit within this paradigm and have proven helpful in our own teaching throughout the years. They are not meant to serve as panaceas for every classroom management issue, but they work enough of the time to be our go-to strategies. Ultimately, the best strategy for *classroom management* is establishing trusting relationships and maintaining a positive and joyful culture in the classroom.

REFERENCES

Anderson, L. (2003). *Cooperative discipline*. Circle Pines, MN: American Guidance Service.
Daniels, H. (2002). *Literature circles: Voice and choice in book clubs & reading groups*. Portland, ME: Stenhouse.
Evertson, C. M., & Weinstein, C. S. (Eds.). (2006). *Handbook of classroom management: Research, practice, and contemporary issues*. Mahwah, NJ: Lawrence Erlbaum.

Chapter Nineteen

Classroom Management from an Organizational Perspective: Positive Behavioral Supports at the System, School, and Staff Levels

Howard M. Knoff

The bell rings. It is 10:20 a.m., and a thousand middle school adolescents of all sizes and shapes pour into South Middle School's (a pseudonym) hallways for the five minutes of chaos that goes with their transition from one classroom to the next. Ignoring the expressionless faces of the staff who are "supervising" this school ritual, the students are in their own worlds and on their own terms—generating a cacophony of mindless chatter, good-natured ribbing, deliberate ridicule, and ego-shattering harassment.

During the five-minute frenzy, some students are celebrated and idolized, some are accepted and supported, some are ignored or rejected, and some are bullied, harassed, and intimidated. As in generations past, there are the emerging class superstars and supermodels, the cool kids, the preps, the brains, the jocks, the thespians, the geeks, the nerds, the losers, the Goths, the punks, the greasers, the burnouts and, of course, just the average students fighting to fit in.

Most troubling, however, is that the largest part of this inner-city middle school's frenzy reflects a school that is out of control. In the bathrooms and hallways, there are ongoing verbal and physical assaults to the degree that some students refuse to use the bathrooms during the day, and some staff avoid the hallways because they then would be responsible for breaking up the fights. Discipline referrals to the office numbered over 3,000 in the first semester of the school year, classroom instruction was virtually nonexistent, and school administrators spent more time responding to discipline problems than preventing them.

In a larger sense, South Middle School had lost control over its own success and destiny. Because it has been cyclically abandoned and micromanaged by the district, staff morale was low and inconsistency was high. Staff turnover was massive—both during and at the end of each school year. And even the state had irresponsibly turned the other cheek by not holding the school and district accountable through eight years of failure and School Improvement status.

WHEN CLASSROOM MANAGEMENT REFLECTS ORGANIZATIONAL MANAGEMENT

South Middle School is a real school—one that, in our experience, similarly exists in other urban, suburban, and rural school districts across the country. In some schools, an effective teacher with an engaging style and curriculum, good student relationships and rapport, and sound classroom instruction and management skills might be able to transcend the conditions noted above. But in most schools, this is not the case. That is because classroom climate reflects school climate, school climate reflects staff climate, and staff climate reflects systems climate.

Yes, South Middle School is a real school that, like hundreds of other schools over the last 30 years, we have been asked to help save and turn around. While the job is not yet finished, we have worked with countless troubled and failing schools and districts across the country since 1990 using our evidence-based school improvement program, Project ACHIEVE (Knoff & Batsche, 1995; Knoff, Finch, & Carlyon, 2004; www.projectachieve.info).

Recognized in 2000 by the U.S. Department of Health & Human Service's Substance Abuse and Mental Health Services Administration (SAMH-SA) as an evidence-based model prevention program, Project ACHIEVE consists of seven interdependent school effectiveness components:

- The *Strategic Planning and Organizational Analysis and Development Component* focuses on strengthening the organizational climate, administrative style, and staff decision-making processes in a school—culminating in an annual School Improvement Plan.
- The *Effective School, Schooling, and Professional Development Component* focuses on the evidence-based professional development, clinical supervision, and evaluation practices that facilitate effective and differentiated instruction and effective and positive behavior management in every classroom.

- The *Academic Instruction and Intervention, or Positive Academic Supports and Services (PASS) Component* focuses on ensuring that every classroom provides effective, differentiated instruction with early intervention services for struggling students.
- The *Behavioral Instruction and Intervention (PBSS) Component* focuses on implementing a comprehensive Positive Behavioral Support System within a school resulting in classrooms with effective classroom management and early intervention services for challenging students.
- The *Problem Solving, Teaming, and Consultation Processes Component* focuses on the multitiered Response to Instruction and Intervention (RtI^2) continuum of services, supports, strategies, and programs for struggling and challenging students.
- The *Parent and Community Training, Support, and Outreach Component* focuses on school-to-community outreach and increasing the involvement of all parents, but especially the involvement of parents of at-risk, underachieving, and chronically nonperforming students.
- The *Data Management, Evaluation, and Accountability Component* focuses on evaluating the status and progress of students' academic and behavioral mastery of information and skills, as well as evaluating the success of the school improvement activities in the other Project ACHIEVE components above.

As outside consultants working with the South Middle School staff, we began the turnaround process by focusing on the following four components: (a) Strategic Planning and Organizational Analysis and Development; (b) Problem Solving, Teaming, and Consultation Processes; and (c) Behavioral Instruction Linked to Behavioral Assessment, Intervention, and Self-Management—also known as the multitiered Positive Behavioral Support System (PBSS) component. Clearly, the fourth component—Data Management, Evaluation, and Accountability was infused into the other three.

PRINCIPLES OF IMPLEMENTATION, INITIAL ACTIONS AND RECOMMENDATIONS

The implementation of Project ACHIEVE was not a random process. In contrast to some school reform and school-wide discipline efforts that do not systematically apply the science of strategic planning, school and classroom management, and student self-management to their policies, procedures, and practices (Knoff, 2012), a clear, evidence-based protocol was used to organize and guide our efforts.

At its core, this protocol uses a data-based, functional assessment, problem solving process to identify the underlying reasons why targeted problems are occurring, linking them to strategic or intensive services, supports, strategies, or programs (Knoff, 2012; Knoff & Dyer, 2013). Below are the principles, and then some of our initial actions and recommendations as we helped this school plan and execute critical and needed system, school, staff, and student changes.

Principle 1: Don't Fight a Ground War Without Air Support

There are two fundamental points here. First, while the national emphasis has been on *school-wide* positive behavioral supports over the years, districts need to set the tone at the elementary and secondary levels respectively, relative to behavioral expectations, standards, and policies; implementation models, training, and supervision; and services, supports, and strategies.

This needs to occur through blended top-down and bottom-up (district-to-school-and-back) shared leadership partnerships and approaches. When this occurs, everything—problem solving, professional development, implementation, and evaluation—becomes more consistent and effective, as well as more time- and cost-efficient.

Second, schools need to be actively supported by their districts. To the extent that school climate and safety, classroom discipline and behavior management, and student interactions and self-management reflect the community, a systems perspective is crucial. But even when individual schools have specific problems in these areas, school and district collaboration, shared responsibility, and targeted planning is more effective than isolating the school, bad-mouthing the staff, and blaming the students.

Documented Practices

South Middle School was one of many middle schools in a district with high levels of student poverty and mobility. Indeed, during a typical school year, 40% of the students moved in or out of South to other middle schools—most often within the same district. Given this, we applied the principle above by meeting with district administrators, encouraging them to begin a secondary-level initiative where all of the district's middle schools would adopt the same core academic curricula and PBSS approaches.

If implemented, we knew that the shared courses and consistent discipline, behavior management, and self-management approaches across the schools would help (a) students to transition when moving from one middle school to the next; (b) staff transferring to new middle school assignments—for example, at the end of the school year—to assimilate more quickly into the new schools' programs, procedures, and instruction; and (c) the district relative to more consistent and cost-effective training, supervision, and evaluation—resulting in stronger staff and student outcomes in these important areas.

Unfortunately, the district's administrators did not pursue this initiative. While that was their prerogative, they also provided no alternative, district-level PBSS guidance or supports. Instead, the district viewed each middle school as an independent entity, and they evaluated the respective administrators on their ability to solve their own problems—despite using an inflexible per pupil expenditure approach that funded each school with no provisions for supplemental discretionary money.

This left the students and staff at South Middle School largely on their own, at the whim of the district's administrative approaches, and frustrated at the district's rigidity on the one hand and its criticism of the school's history of failure on the other. In the end, both students and staff resigned themselves to simply survive another school year.

Principle 2: Begin with the End in Mind

This principle, coined by Stephen Covey (1989), emphasizes the importance of knowing your short-term and long-term outcomes at the beginning of any strategic planning, classroom management, or behavioral intervention initiative. Critically, all outcomes need to be observable, measurable, and attainable, and they need to describe the expected or desired behaviors that will resolve any situation at hand.

Thus, when staff are focused on decreasing or eliminating different inappropriate student behaviors, they also must target the appropriate student behaviors that need to be established, increased, and/or sustained. This is because the absence of the problem does not necessarily represent the presence of a skill (Knoff, 2012). In other words, just because students are not exhibiting behavior problems in a classroom or school, that does not mean that they have learned or mastered the appropriate behaviors that they need to demonstrate.

Documented Practices

In a broad sense, for South Middle School's students, *appropriate student behavior* was defined as their ability to learn, master, and independently apply—in the classroom and common areas of the school—social, emotional, and behavioral self-management skills. Collectively, some of the social skills that were important included listening, communication and conversation, cooperation, negotiation, peer refusal, help seeking, validation and reinforcement, and accepting responsibility skills.

Some of the emotional skills included an awareness of one's own and others' feelings, the ability to manage or cope with different types and intensities of feelings, being able to make positive self-statements that reinforce a constructive sense of self, and the ability to read and understand others' emotional reactions or perspectives. Finally, some of the behavioral skills included how to follow directions, ignore distractions, and respond to teasing, losing, or rejection; acknowledge, apologize for, and accept consequences; avoid difficult peer or emotionally volatile situations, and respond positively and appropriately to peer pressure.

While the scientifically based components needed to teach these skills are described below, the last facet of the *end in mind* involves our definition of *mastery*. This definition holds that students have mastered skills or behaviors when they are able to demonstrate them under "conditions of emotionality" (Knoff, 2012). Thus, students have mastered their social, emotional, and behavioral self-management skills not just when they can demonstrate them during times of calm and stability, but during times when things are demanding, stressful, chaotic, or traumatic.

Principle 3: If You Don't Know Where You're Going, Any Road Will Get You There

This principle suggests two things. First, school discipline, classroom management, and student self-management approaches should not be implemented in a random, experimental, or uninformed fashion. Critically, an integrated set of sound, scientifically-established principles and practices already exists in these areas at the school, staff, and student levels (Knoff, 2012). These principles and practices have been organized into a *road map* that provides a school with different options or pathways toward eventual success.

Second, while science should guide practice, strategic planning at the school level and data-based problem solving at the school and student levels best determine which specific services, supports, strategies, or programs are needed by a school to maximize its success. Strategic planning and data-based problem solving, then, provide the GPS guidance that helps schools determine which *roads* are needed as they navigate through current, expected, and targeted situations and circumstances.

When random approaches are used, success rarely results, and students and staff become resistant to new approaches because the previous ones have not worked. Thus, interventions must be systematically chosen so that they have the highest probability of success. To do this, the data-based problem solving process must be used to determine the underlying reasons that explain why a specific behavioral problem is occurring.

Once validated, these reasons are linked to the right instructional or intervention approaches that then must be implemented with integrity and the right degree of intensity. For example, there may be many reasons why a student or group of students persistently tease or taunt selected peers. If we don't assess and validate the predominant reason(s), then our interventions will not successfully change the behavior. In fact, the wrong intervention may strengthen or worsen the inappropriate behavior and make it more resistant to future change. This principle occurs, again, at the school, staff, and student levels.

Documented Practices

At South Middle School, Project ACHIEVE's evidence-based PBSS blueprint for school safety, classroom management, and student self-management was used to guide the strategic planning and data-based problem solving process. This blueprint integrates five interdependent domains at the prevention, strategic intervention, and crisis management/intensive need levels (see Figure 19.1).

The first domain includes activities that establish and sustain positive classroom and school climates, largely by developing strong staff-to-staff, staff-to-student, and student-to-student relationships. The second domain involves the identification of explicit, observable pro-social classroom and school common area expectations that are directly taught to all students using an evidence-based social, emotional, and/or behavioral skills instruction program. This program includes the school's mental health professionals who work with more challenging students at the strategic intervention and crisis management/intensive need levels (Knoff, 2012).

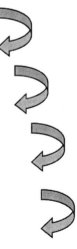

Positive Climates and Prosocial Relationships

Expectations and Skill Instruction: Teach
  Social, Emotional, and Behavioral Skills

Motivation/Accountability: Motivate Appropriate
  Behavior, and Hold Students Accountable for
  Inappropriate Behavior

Maintain Consistency: Within and Across Students,
  Staff, Settings, Circumstances, and Situations

Apply to Special Situations: Common Areas of
  the School, and Teasing, Taunting, Bullying,
  Harassment, Hazing, and Physical Aggression
  Peer Interactions

Figure 19.1.   The Positive Behavioral Support System (PBSS) Model: Evidence-based Components (Source: www.projectachieve.info)

The third component involves the development and use of school-wide student motivation and accountability systems (called Behavioral Matrices) that identify (a) expected student behaviors, connecting them with positive responses, incentives, and rewards; and (b) different *intensity levels* of inappropriate behaviors, connecting them with research-based responses and interventions that help decrease or eliminate these behaviors while establishing and increasing the expected behaviors.

Finally, the last two components focus on (a) holding staff and students accountable for *consistently* implementing the first three PBSS components across different situations and circumstances, and (b) applying these components in the common areas of the school and to help the prevention of and early response to individual students and groups of students involved in teasing, taunting, bullying, harassment, hazing, and/or physical aggression.

To begin the strategic planning and data-based problem solving process, we completed a number of needs assessment and resource mapping activities early in our consultation. In fact, during our initial meeting with the faculty, we got them into small cross-disciplinary and vertical grade-level groups, and asked them to identify student, staff, and school strengths and assets, weaknesses and limitations, barriers and threats, and resources and opportunities respectively.

We also asked them to identify the most significant staff and student problems in the school. These discussions were continued during the next few months in different staff PLC (professional learning community) meetings as we moved from problem identification and analysis to intervention generation and implementation. Relative to the students, a series of one hour semi-structured focus group discussions with randomly selected students from different grades, programs, and backgrounds were conducted to elicit their perceptions of the school, staff, and peers, along with their concerns and possible solutions.

Eventually, all of the staff and student concerns were clarified, prioritized, and analyzed in the context of the PBSS blueprint described above. In the end, both the students and the staff expressed their distress with the school's (a) pervasive, negative school-wide culture; (b) gang and racial prejudice issues; (c) poorly maintained bathrooms where rats frequently roamed; (d) unsafe and crowded hallways where teasing, bullying, and fights were commonplace; (e) high turnover rates of administrators, teachers, and other staff, resulting in inconsistent classroom instruction and school discipline; and (f) lack of student management resulting in some classrooms where students were intimidating teachers and disrupting others' educational opportunities.

These concerns then were prioritized, and an integrated intervention plan was developed that described the school's initial goals, objectives, and desired outcomes; the interventions or approaches needed to achieve these outcomes; the resources, training, and supervision needed to implement the interventions; and the short-term and long-term evaluation approaches needed to determine whether the interventions actually worked. Critically, the intervention plan initially focused on stabilizing the school given its current unstable, unpredictable, and crisis-oriented status. This impact of this decision is discussed in Principle 4 below.

Principle 4: Sometimes You Need to Stabilize in Order to Mobilize

As referenced above, from an organizational perspective, there are times when an environment or setting is so unstable that it is unwise to begin implementing a more goal-directed intervention plan. When this occurs, fast and effective crisis management actions are needed that involve resources and strategies typically not considered or used under normal circumstances.

As these actions unfold, it is essential to overestimate the resources needed so that they fully cover the situation and that leaders communicate directly and consistently with students, staff, and district personnel—along with parents, community responders, other community leaders, and the media.

Documented Practices

In the end, a series of targeted recommendations designed primarily to stabilize the school were made to South Middle School's administration and School Leadership Team. These included the following:

1. immediately cleaning up the school and addressing the bathroom problems;
2. organizing the staff supervision in the hallways and instituting a *hallway sweep* system to get students to class on time;
3. implementing a "behavior matrix" accountability system that identified expected student behaviors along with different intensities of inappropriate behavior and teacher or administrator responses respectively;
4. identifying, analyzing, and immediately addressing the "frequent flyer" students who were presenting the most significant and/or persistent disciplinary problems;
5. working with the school's formal and informal student leaders, implementing a plan where they guided their peers toward more prosocial behaviors;
6. reasserting the consequences across the school for teasing, taunting, bullying, harassment, hazing, and fighting, focusing especially on cybergossip and cyberbullying, and instituting an anonymous "early warning referral" system for students;

7. training or retraining support staff and noninstructional personnel on the behavioral expectations at the bus stops, on the buses, and on the playground used by students before school and after lunch; and

8. hiring a cadre of permanent classroom substitute teachers for the remainder of the school year, and training and supervising them on instructional and classroom management skills.

Principle 5: Individual Leaders Promote Change, Shared Leadership Achieves It

This last principle emphasizes the importance of formal and informal shared leadership approaches and structures within a school. While many, especially secondary, schools still utilize an assistant principal or dean as the only individual responsible for discipline, this person's leadership needs to be shared by a representative group of staff who meet on a regular basis and are collectively responsible for functionally implementing the PBSS as well as other related annual goals and objectives.

When functioning effectively, the representatives on this PBSS or School Climate and Discipline Committee become important facilitators who communicate and help to address teacher-level concerns at the school or systems level and, conversely, who share and encourage their colleagues to implement school-level services, supports, programs, and other initiatives at the classroom levels.

Documented Practices

A *School Discipline/PBSS Committee* was established early on at South Middle School. Over time, this committee became responsible for implementing and evaluating activities related to the school's (a) social climate and staff-to-student interactions, (b) discipline and behavior management programs, (c) school safety and crisis intervention processes, and (d) other PBSS initiatives.

The committee also examined the most effective ways to teach, infuse, and facilitate students' use of positive interpersonal, social problem solving, conflict prevention and resolution, and social, emotional, and behavioral coping skills and interactions, with a goal of helping students to feel more connected to the school, engaged in classroom instruction, and safe across the common areas of the school.

Additionally, the School Discipline/PBSS Committee became responsible for addressing large-scale issues of teasing, taunting, bullying, harassment, hazing, and physical aggression—working to prevent these situations across the school and student body and helping to develop responses when they occurred. Finally, this committee worked to involve the school's support staff (e.g., custodians, cafeteria workers, secretaries, bus drivers) in its efforts, and it reached out to parents, community agencies, and other community leaders in collaborative efforts to extend PBSS activities and outcomes to home and community settings.

CONCLUSION

While our work at South Middle School continues, we have seen many positive effects. The classrooms and common school areas now are far more orderly, positive, and safe. Student and staff interactions are also more positive and appropriate, and a greater degree of consistency is evident. Finally, students are far more academically engaged, and academic achievement appears to be on the rise.

We believe that the system, school, staff, and student perspectives described in this chapter were essential to this progress. Peter Drucker (1967) said, "The best way to predict the future is to create it." We must create (or recreate) a 21st century approach to school discipline that incorporates the evidence-based road map discussed. The roads that you take for your classroom or school in this area now are up to you.

Author's Note

This chapter is based on material and published works copyrighted by Project ACHIEVE Press, Little Rock, AR 72212. As such, the material in this chapter is covered under those previous copyrights.

REFERENCES

Covey, S. R. (1989). *The 7 habits of highly effective people.* New York, NY: Simon and Schuster.

Drucker, P. (1967). *The effective executive.* New York, NY: Harper & Row.

Knoff, H. M. (2012). *School discipline, classroom management, and student self-management: A Positive Behavioral Support implementation guide.* Thousand Oaks, CA: Corwin Press.

Knoff, H. M., & Batsche, G. M. (1995). Project ACHIEVE: Analyzing a school reform process for at-risk and underachieving students. *School Psychology Review, 24,* 579–603.

Knoff, H. M., & Dyer, C. (2013). *RtI²—Response to Instruction and Intervention: Implementing successful academic and behavioral intervention systems.* Rexford, NY: International Center for Leadership in Education.

Knoff, H. M., Finch, C., & Carlyon, W. (2004). Inside Project ACHIEVE: A comprehensive, research-proven whole school improvement process focused on student academic and behavioral outcomes. In K. Robinson (Ed.), *Advances in school-based mental health: Best practices and program models* (pp. 19–28). Kingston, NJ: Civic Research Institute.

Chapter Twenty

Twenty-First Century Classroom Management: It Is Time for a New Perspective

Marie Menna Pagliaro

SOCIETAL CHANGES IN THE 21ST CENTURY

There is no doubt that our society is changing rapidly. Information continues to explode. Our classes are growing in social, emotional, cultural, and academic diversity, making them more inclusive and heterogeneous.

Beginning in 1991, the Secretary's Commission on Achieving Necessary Skills (of the U.S. Department of Labor) studied what changes would be expected in 21st-century society. They concluded that people will be changing jobs approximately every five years and that the demands of these new jobs will require skills associated with team membership, listening, self-management, time management, assuming responsibility, and following schedules.

States are currently attempting to revamp education to meet the demands of the 21st century by including life skills, a wide range of intellectual skills, and social skills. There is agreement between leaders in both industry and academia that students have to learn to become innovative, solve problems, and interact successfully with people from many different cultures (Gewertz, 2008).

LAUREN BULLOCK STRUGGLES WITH CHANGE

Lauren Bullock had been teaching fifth grade for eight years. During that time she became increasingly aware of the changes in society and how these

163

changes had to impact what she was doing traditionally in the classroom. Through extensive readings, collaboration with peers, and visiting classrooms in other districts, she came to realize how interconnected curriculum, instruction, and classroom management are and that it was necessary for her to modify her approach to all three.

At first, she was hesitant about moving away from the security of her established ways. But gradually over a three-year period, after fighting the tendency to revert to old habits and frustrated with mistakes along the way, her teaching has evolved to a delivery that is radically different. She believes that after struggling through so many changes, she is finally on her way to becoming a full-fledged 21st-century classroom manager.

LAUREN'S NEW PLAN

Currently, before the school year begins, Lauren goes out of the way to check her new students' records to determine the content they are ready to learn before she plans curriculum. This information helps her avoid problems immediately by not offering content that is too easy or too difficult.

On the first day of school, and *every* day, Lauren, using direct eye contact, greets each student as she or he enters the room with comments like, "Hi," "Good morning," "How are you today?" "Nice backpack." As she learns the students' names, she includes their names in the greeting. This acknowledgment makes the students aware that they are recognized and noticed. She arranges an activity where the students get to know each other's names. Then the students follow through by always addressing each other by name during class.

Lauren already has a seating chart prepared so she is able to assign the students seats. Then she promptly begins class this way: "We are in this together. When one of us succeeds, we all succeed. When one of us fails, we all fail. It is critically important to me personally that all of us do well." This message is very powerful.

ESTABLISHING RULES AND PROCEDURES

Of course, Lauren realizes that she must implement the message she conveyed on the first day consistently. So she follows through by having her students participate in establishing both rules and procedures. She explains that a rule conveys a general expectation that can be applied in many different circumstances (e.g., "Listen when others are speaking") and a procedure states a course of action for a routine such as a method for passing out or collecting materials.

Together with her students, Lauren then determines rules. There is shared responsibility for implementing and enforcing rules, which includes determining rewards for following and consequences for not following rules. The rules are reasonable, clear, short, minimal, and posted. When necessary, procedures (clearing aisles, lining up) are rehearsed.

Lauren takes the time to explain rules and procedures and why they are important so that her students understand them. This clarification is especially critical for her students whose cultures may not be compatible with rules and procedures normally implemented in American classrooms. However, she is careful not to spend too much time on rules, procedures, or explanations because she wants to set the tone for the year by beginning with an engaging activity.

CREATING A POSITIVE CLASSROOM ENVIRONMENT

The classroom atmosphere Lauren attempts to establish is warm, friendly, and caring. All members have mutual respect for and support each other so that everyone has a stake in the success of all other members. This environment provides physical and emotional safety, making her classroom a place where students feel they can take risks, ask questions, answer questions, make mistakes, admit they do not know an answer, or come up with an "out-of-the-box" idea without negative comments from any class member. There is zero tolerance for derogatory comments or bullying (Pagliaro, 2011).

Lauren makes it a point to never talk above students' voices while giving directions or conducting instruction, for a contemporary classroom manager wants to ensure that there is mutual respect among all class members. Both she and the students show respect for each other by listening to each other.

Even though the common threads of (a) student input; (b) student autonomy, control, and involvement; (c) shared responsibility; and (d) sense of community are incorporated into all aspects of managing her classroom, she is keenly aware that she is ultimately responsible for the behavior and progress of all her students.

CURRICULUM AND INSTRUCTION

Lauren knows that her curriculum and instruction have to reflect the needs of the 21st century. Therefore, in addition to her own goals, Lauren invites her students to add their own curriculum goals. She gives them structured choices: How will they learn? What opportunities will there be to self-reflect and monitor their goal achievement? How can they redirect their effort, when necessary? How will they play an essential role in their own assessment/evaluation?

The choices are authentic, mutually acceptable, and offered for behavior as well as for instruction. Providing choices communicates to students that they are competent and responsible. It also helps students to practice decision making, allows opportunities for students to exhibit their accomplishments and helps them learn that school is pertinent to their lives.

Her students are involved in relevant experiences, authentic problems, and as fifth graders, are mature enough to participate in constructing scoring rubrics. Depending on the situation, students may work independently or in groups, check each other's work, and coach when warranted, with all individual members taking responsibility for the group's achievements and supporting each other to attain success.

When it comes to instruction, Lauren relies less on lectures and sequential lessons and more on active, project-based, hands-on learning (Pagliaro, 2012). She believes that in this environment students learn skills and concepts that can be applied outside of school.

She uses primary sources, inside as well as outside resources, and technology as opposed to the textbook or worksheets as predominant instructional materials. Her students are encouraged to create things; to read good books; to choose some readings themselves; to have fun together; and to show off their work. They are even given time to tinker.

GROUP WORK

Lauren has avoided many problem behaviors by keeping whole-class instruction to a minimum and focusing more on group work, especially after an initial lesson has been introduced. When she does teach a lesson—whether to a group or to the whole class—she does so with enthusiasm, always noting how her excitement is picked up by the students.

To facilitate successful group work, Lauren makes sure that students within each group have assigned responsibilities. Students have input regarding what these responsibilities should be and how to implement them. They are clarified and practiced so that all students know what to do regarding their assignment, how each member will contribute to that assignment, and how to handle any problems that may occur.

HANDLING TRANSITION TIME

One problem in particular that one of her prior classes had noted involved disruptions that occurred during transitions, especially when changing activities after working in groups. After doing some research (Wong & Wong, 2005), Lauren advised her class that she would give them a verbal cue a few minutes ahead of time that a transition was coming and restate at that time what she expected them to do during the transition. When the time actually came, she would signal them with a bell, light flickering, music playing, or rhythmic hand clapping.

After the students had actually performed the transition, Lauren complimented those who cooperated with expected procedures. She had the next assignment ready and, when the students were all in place, gave them another signal that it was time to begin. Now this process has become routine and if it or any other routine does not work with present or future classes, Lauren is ready for their suggestions to improve the process.

CULTURE AND EMPATHY

In the culturally diverse 21st century classroom, Lauren is genuinely curious about different cultures represented by her students. She asks students to share their customs with the class and capitalizes on these customs during instruction. She also tries to demonstrate that she has heard and understands students' feelings by paraphrasing some of their comments made in frustration or anger. For instance, if a student says, "I hate math," Lauren might say, "You're having difficulty solving this problem" (paraphrase). Then she would add, "Let's see if we can work together to solve it."

She moves about the room freely and frequently so that she is in contact with all students. When necessary, Lauren, together with her students, reminds misbehaving students of the rules to which they have all agreed and that their behavior is not supporting other class members, thus interfering with the learning of others. She most often reminds misbehavers by continuing instruction without interruption, while simultaneously pointing to the rule not being followed, which is listed on the poster developed the first day of class.

Lauren makes a sincere effort to implement the *power of positive* by maintaining a constructive atmosphere in her class. One way she does this is by making learning personal. She makes it a point to find out something personal about each student, in particular his or her strengths, and uses this information in instruction. Lauren knows that when students are involved personally, they become more involved emotionally, and that "emotions . . . are not the cards at the game table but the table itself" (Jensen, 2005, p. 80).

Whenever the occasion allows, Lauren offers students the opportunity to talk about themselves (Marzano, 2007). This activity provides another instance that involves students emotionally in learning, especially when she connects what she knows about them personally and/or their interests to the knowledge and skills to be studied.

When a student accomplishes a task, Lauren is sure to offer encouragement. This she does by sending "You" messages which emphasize positives the students have performed. In her readings she was reminded that this technique is opposite the one delivered in the past, where a teacher sent an "I" message which communicates teacher control by indicating what the teacher thinks or feels. Instead, Lauren believes that students should feel positive about what they have achieved and what control they have taken in applying their own effort. Yet, as a collaborator in the classroom, if an appropriate occasion should arise, Lauren retains the right to express her feelings about what is happening at that time and how it affects her.

In promoting a positive classroom environment, Lauren remains aware of her own behavior. She tries to exhibit a sense of humor, which is easy for her. This makes teaching less stressful with students enjoying her classes more. If unanticipated humorous events occur in the classroom, Lauren is willing to laugh, even at herself, which shows that she is comfortable with herself and with her students.

Lauren establishes a positive but realistic level of expectation, not only for behavior but also for academics. She never gives up on any student for she knows that the confidence she exhibits will often give students the extra incentive they may need.

She understands that successful people can often trace their success, or possibly their redirection in life, to the fact that one person, usually a teacher, believed in them and encouraged them, especially with the support of the class. It is awesome for Lauren to feel that she has the potential to be that person. She is particularly concerned with any student who may be a loner and is constantly alert and quick to involve that student with others in a significant way.

As a shared leader and learning partner, Lauren never loses sight of the fact that she is a role model, a critical role model for her students. She attempts to behave as a mature person they can look up to by using proper speech and grammar and by dressing professionally. She models flexibility by trying out new teaching strategies, new materials, and new activities.

If she makes a mistake or does not know the answer to a question, Lauren admits it. This behavior on her part demonstrates that she is a person who takes responsibility, thereby providing a good example for her students. They respect her more for her admission. She conveys the message that it is all right to make mistakes. We all do, and what is most noteworthy about mistakes is that we learn from them and try to do better; mistakes help us grow. And if we do not know the answer to a question, what is even more important is that we learn how to find the answer.

Lauren attempts to interact with her students in a friendly (not over-friendly) but businesslike manner. She remembers that she does not have to be loved by her students but has to be respected. In turn, she treats her students with respect, noting that they like teachers who are trusting, caring, and respectful. And teachers who are liked have more influence on students and have a better chance of gaining their cooperation.

Lauren always tries to be firm but fair. She keeps her promises and avoids reprimanding the entire class when only a few are responsible for misbehavior. When some students are misbehaving, she has the class first discuss the misbehavior and then determine what should be done about it before she intervenes. One method that she has found particularly effective is having a misbehaving student model the correct behavior for the rest of the class.

In the continuing spirit of involving students in classroom management, Lauren asks for their suggestions regarding what signals they might give her when they feel that they "got it" and what activities they can recommend during free or unstructured time, which is conducive to off-task behavior. Typically, these times occur when students enter the room, when she takes the roll, or when students finish their work ahead of time.

For these occasions, Lauren, after negotiating with her students, offers "sponge" activities, substantive learning activities that absorb free time. Sponge activities may include reading a book, working on a computer program, completing a project at the learning activity center, or completing a warm-up assignment that is written on the board (Boynton & Boynton, 2005).

In her attempt to bond with all students and ensure that all students feel bonded with each other, Lauren shows that she is interested in her students as people. She has personal "chats" with each student to find out more about him or her and what together can be done to make him or her successful. Occasionally, she continues her personal and positive approach by recognizing something personal or positive in each student.

Statements Lauren has used such as, "You wear a lot of bright shirts," or, "You've shown great improvement in your computation skills," go a long way in keeping her and her students connected. When a student behaves well consistently or accomplishes a challenging task for his or her performance level, Lauren acknowledges these achievements by communicating with the student's home by calling, sending an e-mail, or sending a note.

Lauren's learning environment provides opportunities for all to achieve. She teaches for success, conveying a pervasive expectation of progress. This success stimulates further motivation to achieve and reduces the desire for students to become disruptive. When students are meaningfully and actively occupied, Lauren takes pictures of them and displays their pictures on the bulletin board and in the hallway with an appropriate title such as, "We Are Great," or "We're Almost There." She knows that hard work gives students a feeling of accomplishment.

Through self-reflection, Lauren wants to make sure that she does not submit her students to negative behaviors that she herself witnessed from teachers when she was a student. She is careful to avoid sarcasm and ridicule, favoritism, making a big deal over minor issues, or carrying a grudge. She constantly facilitates the free and open interchange of ideas and suggestions so that she can steer clear of authoritarian tactics to which she herself was subjected.

Most important, Lauren makes sure that she is consistent so that her students will feel secure. They know what to expect when a question is asked, when they have to ask permission to perform a certain activity, and when they have to ask how to complete assignments. Lauren distinguishes between consistency and inflexibility, for there may be times when she needs to reflect on procedures and change, with student feedback, those that may not be effective.

One of the most enlightening activities Lauren engages in with her class is videotaping them periodically. Then she lets them view the video so that they can discuss how their work habits were successful or how productivity/behavior could be improved. She also asks the students to evaluate her and notes what changes she might make in her own performance.

MOVING ON

As Lauren continues to grow as a 21st-century classroom manager, she is serving as a consultant for other teachers in her school. She understands that they will first have to modify their attitude just as she did before transitioning from complete class control to shared leadership. Then, while keeping the same student-centric thrust she uses, they may have to adjust her fifth-grade approach to some degree, according to the grade and student maturation level with which they are dealing.

Lauren has become an advocate for her new methodology, realizing that it will not be as effective unless it is adopted school-wide and system-wide. And that, as Lauren already is aware of, will be her most significant challenge.

Author's Note

All names are pseudonyms.

REFERENCES

Boynton, M., & Boynton, C. (2005). *The educator's guide to preventing and solving discipline problems*. Alexandria, VA: ASCD.

Gewertz, C. (2008, October 15). States press ahead on 21st-century skills. *Education Week, 28*(8), 21, 23.

Jensen, E. (2005). *Teaching with the brain in mind* (2nd ed.). Alexandria, VA: ASCD.

Marzano, R. (2007). *The art and science of teaching: A comprehensive framework for effective instruction*. Alexandria, VA: ASCD.

Pagliaro, M. (2011). *Educator or bully: Managing the 21st century classroom.* Lanham, MD: Rowman & Littlefield Education.

Pagliaro, M. (2012). *Research-based unit and lesson planning: Maximizing student achievement.* Lanham, MD: Rowman & Littlefield Education.

Secretary's Commission on Achieving Necessary Skills. (1991). *What work requires of schools: A SCANS report for America 2000.* Washington, DC: U.S. Department of Labor.

Wong, H., & Wong, R. (2005, September). *Effective teaching: A successful first day is no secret.* Retrieved from http://teachers.net/wong/SEP05

Afterword

Building Resiliency in Students and Teachers: Key Ideas from Research and Practice

Bryan Harris

Think about someone you know who has experienced a tragedy and has bounced back after the adversity with a renewed sense of purpose and direction. Imagine the person who seems to have a reservoir of internal strength to deal with the challenges of life. In the face of hardship, these people seem to rebound and even thrive despite the challenges. Quite simply, they seem equipped to successfully handle the unexpected events of life.

Now think about someone who has experienced similar challenges only to succumb to the pressures; the demands of life seem to get the best of them. What is the difference between those who can handle the pressures and those who cannot? The individuals who have the capacity to deal with the problems of life have what educators and researchers refer to as resiliency.

WHAT IS RESILIENCY?

Resiliency can be defined as the ability to persist in the face of adversity or the ability to bounce back after facing challenging circumstances. Henderson and Milstein (2003)—in their book *Resiliency in Schools*—stated that "Resilience can be defined as the capacity to spring back, rebound, successfully adapt in the face of adversity, and develop the social and academic competence despite exposure to extreme stress or simply to the stress that is inherent in today's world" (p. 7).

Similarly, Wolin and Wolin (1999), co-directors of Project Resilience, a program that educates families, schools, and communities defined resiliency as, "the process of persisting in the face of adversity" (para. 1).

Resiliency is a collection of skills and abilities that allows an individual to navigate difficult times in life. Building resiliency in students—particularly those who are already struggling in school—is one of the most important responsibilities of a teacher. Time spent helping students to become resilient will have a positive impact on their immediate prospects in school and their long-term success in life (Bernard, 2004).

WHY DO WE NEED RESILIENCY?

When an individual is resilient, they are able to successfully deal with the difficulties they encounter. Life in school, for students and teachers alike, is filled with challenges and obstacles. When facing those hardships, individuals can either persevere or they can fail. Unfortunately, many students are ill equipped to deal with the emotional, academic, and behavioral demands that are inherent with attending school. In addition, beyond the school walls, many students face stresses that can make life, both in and out of school, a challenge.

Both children and adults need what Henderson and Milstein (2003) referred to as a *self-righting* ability in the midst of adversity. Children are increasingly exposed to stresses—within the school, the family, and the larger community—that require skills to cope with those stresses. Children, however, are not alone in their need to develop resiliency.

Schools can be challenging places for adults as well. Krovetz (1998), author of *Fostering Resiliency*, pointed out that schools generally do not build resiliency in either their students or their staff. Students and teachers alike need what Ungar (2008) referred to as a *life preserver* that will help us navigate the difficult times.

RESILIENCY AND CLASSROOM MANAGEMENT

Perhaps the most promising outcome from resiliency research is the fact that it can be learned and developed. There is no greater gift educators can offer their students than to provide them with the ability to handle life's difficulties. Furthermore, there is an obligation, especially with struggling or challenging students, to provide them with skills that will allow them to be successful in classrooms and in society in general. Classroom management—what educators do to manage and organize the learning environment—offers teachers the ideal venue to overtly teach resiliency skills.

Marzano (2003), perhaps more so than any other contemporary author or researcher, has advocated the principle that *what teachers do matters*: how teachers organize and deliver instruction, how they manage and motivate students, and how they engage learners makes a difference in their achievement and behavior.

Following similar assumptions about a teacher's influence, Bernard (2004) found three key characteristics that can foster resiliency in students: (a) caring and supportive adults, (b) positive expectations about ability, and (c) active participation in the life of the classroom and school. Henderson and Milstein (2003) developed a popular program for educators, which outlined six characteristics that help develop resilient students. Their *Resiliency Wheel* includes the actions that teachers should take to develop resiliency in students. Teachers should (a) provide opportunities for meaningful participation, (b) set and communicate high expectations, (c) provide caring and support, (d) increase pro-social bonding, (e) set clear, consistent boundaries, and (f) teach life skills.

KEY IDEAS FROM THE RESEARCH

The seven ideas outlined here offer educators, at the classroom and school level, an opportunity to reflect on practice and consider changes that could positively impact student behavior and achievement while building much-needed resiliency.

1. *Avoid labeling children as "high-risk" or "at-risk."* Instead, refer to high-risk environments or situations that present challenging conditions. All children are capable of learning given the appropriate support and they tend to live up to or down to the expectations we set for them (Ginsburg, 2011).
2. *The person who delivers the program is more important than the program itself.* There are numerous effective programs available that are designed to increase resiliency in students and there is significant research about the effect of teaching students the skills and attitudes of resiliency. However, personal relationships and connections are the foundation of all effective programs (Werner & Smith, 1992).
3. *Sometimes the apple does fall far from the tree.* Students facing challenging situations or difficult home lives need to know and believe that they can succeed. They need to see, through stories, examples, and role models, that with a strong work ethic and commitment they can be successful. They need not be bound solely by their environment, background, or surroundings (Jensen, 2009).

4. *View children not as problems to be fixed but as individuals with strengths, dreams, and opinions.* Traditionally schools have focused on the identification, remediation, and correction of *deficits*. Indeed, schools need to know where students are lacking and work to help them master important skills and content. However, educators also need to focus on the strengths and abilities of students for them to truly thrive and overcome adverse situations (Henderson & Milstein, 2003).

5. *Students must be actively involved in the life of the school and in their own learning.* Resiliency is not developed by being passive. Students need to connect to the people, the content, and the overall learning environment in order to thrive. Teachers can achieve that by challenging students to track their own learning, creating goals, and connecting to other students with similar interests (Rothstein-Fisch & Trumbull, 2008).

6. *Schooling can be cold and impersonal.* The curriculum, the over-reliance on testing, the schedules, and even the instruction can sometimes lead children to believe that school is something that is done *to them*. Kohn (1999) suggested that educators take time to make personal connections with students, laugh with them, and share stories to make school warm, fun, and inviting.

7. *Resiliency is not constant.* Resiliency tends to ebb and flow throughout a person's life based on current situations and challenges. The resilient person is the one who understands and comes to terms with life's difficulties and subsequently bounces back, learns, and even thrives through the tough times (Bernard, 2004).

EVIDENCE-BASED STRATEGIES TO FOSTER RESILIENCY IN STUDENTS

Knowing that what teachers do matters in regards to fostering resiliency, there are specific research-based strategies that are likely to help students develop the skills and attitudes they need to be successful. Because educators are already busy with implementing new standards, administering assessments, and addressing a myriad of other responsibilities, the strategies suggested here may appear to be surprisingly ordinary. That is, they are easy to implement in the classroom setting in conjunction with other classroom activities and plans, yet they are also effective at building resiliency in students.

- *Be optimistic, caring, and empathetic.* Educators need to model the very actions and beliefs that are desired from students. Students are unlikely to internalize a different set of values if they see a disconnect between the way teachers and adults act and the way they expect students to act.

- *Focus on strengths rather than weaknesses.* All students have strengths. Educators are more likely to reach struggling students when the focus is on the strengths students already possess. Express appreciation for uniqueness, talent, and ability. Build upon student interests and strengths to involve them in community service projects and other activities that allow them to see the world beyond their own first-hand experiences.
- *Meet the need for belonging.* All students need to have a sense that they belong to a group. Struggling students particularly need to know that they are more than just another student. They need to know that they are important, that they are essential to the class, and that they would be missed if they were absent. If a student misses several days of school, give them a call at home to ask how they are.
- *Create a high-warmth and low-criticism environment.* Warmth, positiveness, and caring should permeate every aspect of the classroom atmosphere. Students should feel secure in the knowledge that they will be emotionally as well as physically safe in the classroom. Sarcasm, negativity, and a "my way or the highway" approach is unlikely to help create a positive atmosphere of student achievement.
- *Set high, realistic expectations.* Start with the belief that all students are capable of learning at high levels given the appropriate support and guidance. Recall that the Pygmalion Effect (Rosenthal & Jacobson, 1992) tells us that all individuals tend to live up to or down to the expectations placed on them by others. Setting high expectations is as much about what educators expect of themselves as what they expect of children.
- *Provide consistent, specific, positive feedback.* This is among the most powerful tools teachers have at their disposal. Provide feedback to students about their academic achievement as well as their behavior, growth, and progress towards goals.
- *Celebrate successes.* Take the time to comment, notice, and praise students when they are successful at navigating tough challenges. Acknowledge students' success by sharing their stories, writing notes of congratulations, and expressing appreciation for their efforts.
- *Teach conflict resolution skills.* Utilize role play techniques, small group discussions, videos, and real-life scenarios as opportunities for students to practice, in a safe and non-threatening environment, the skills they are being asked to develop. Play "what if" games and challenge students to think through how they could react to difficult situations.
- *Communicate positively with caretakers.* Parents and families of struggling students typically get very little positive communication from school. Parents and students alike expect all the news from school to be focused on problems and deficiencies. Reverse this trend and communi-

cate positively with families about their children. Do this on a regular basis to build trust and relationships.

STRATEGIES TO FOSTER RESILIENCE IN EDUCATORS

As educators, we need to be aware of our own resiliency and ability to handle the stresses inherent with the job. Schools are not places that typically foster or support resiliency in either their students or their educators. For teachers, schools can be stressful, hectic, unforgiving, and sometimes painful places. In order to properly take care of students, we must also take care of ourselves. Knowing that healthy, well-balanced educators are necessary to create healthy, well-balanced students, the following strategies are offered.

- *Take care of your health.* Many educators are stressed out to the point that they skip sleep, eat a poor diet, and fail to exercise on a regular basis. While teaching is the most noble and important of professions, educators should not sacrifice their health or their family in the pursuit of teaching.
- *Avoid complaining.* Grumbling about students, about the system, about what should be or should not be is typically a waste of time. There is no such thing as a perfect organization and the grass is rarely greener on the other side. Take action where you have control and seek positive influence where you can make a difference. Complaining and whining about problems typically adds more stress to life, not less.
- *Deal with conflict.* When difficult issues or situations arise, deal with them quickly and honestly. Don't let conflicts fester and grow without a plan to rapidly deal with them. Worrying about problems, complaining about co-workers or students, and stressing out about disagreements typically takes more of a toll on you than it does on anyone else.
- *Control your calendar.* Create time for family, friends, exercise, and fun activities. Those things in life that are a priority should be placed on the calendar and made a priority. Living a balanced, resilient life begins by taking control of time.
- *Develop a professional support network.* Because teaching can be stressful and demanding, all educators need a positive support network of colleagues who understand and can provide guidance and advice. Meet with them regularly to share ideas, brainstorm plans, and discuss the challenges of the profession.
- *Find a professional passion.* Keeping up with best practices, research, and trends can be a challenge for busy educators. One of the best ways to stay current is to find and cultivate a professional passion. Dive in and become an expert in that area and share ideas, strategies, and techniques with your colleagues.

- *Foster a sense of humor.* What we do as educators is serious business. While the job mandates a level of professionalism, we also need to have fun. Make it a goal to share a laugh every day with students and look for the opportunities to truly enjoy the job.
- *Remember to ask for help when you need it.* Asking for assistance is a sign of strength, not weakness. When the demands of the job seem overwhelming, seek out the help from your professional support network, from parents, from friends, and even from students. We expect students to seek assistance and help when they need it, as educators we should do the same.
- *Find an outlet.* Strive to live a balanced life that includes time spent doing things that are joyful, fun, and personally fulfilling. Develop a hobby, passion, or interest separate from education and do not feel guilty about devoting time to it.

CONCLUSION

As educators, we have an obligation to assist our students in developing the traits, personal characteristics, and abilities they need in order to be successful in life. Resiliency, that essential skill set that allows us to navigate the tough times in life, is one of those obligations. The good news is that resilience can be learned and teachers have at their disposal effective strategies that can help both students and themselves acquire and expand on their capacities.

REFERENCES

Bernard, B. (2004). *Resiliency: What we have learned.* San Francisco, CA: WestEd.

Ginsburg, K. (2011). *Building resilience in children and teens.* Elk Grove Village, IL. American Academy of Pediatrics.

Henderson, N., & Milstein, M. (2003). *Resiliency in schools: Making it happen for students and educators* (2nd ed.). Thousand Oaks, CA: Corwin Press.

Jensen, E. (2009). *Teaching with poverty in mind.* Alexandria, VA: ASCD.

Kohn, A. (1999). *The schools our children deserve.* New York, NY: Houghton Mifflin.

Krovetz, M. (1998). *Fostering resiliency: Expecting all students to use their minds and hearts well.* Thousand Oaks, CA: Corwin Press.

Marzano, R. (2003). *Classroom management that works.* Alexandria, VA: ASCD.

Rosenthal, R., & Jacobson, L. (1992). *Pygmalion in the classroom* (Expanded ed.). New York, NY: Irvington.

Rothstein-Fisch, C., & Trumbull, E. (2008). *Managing diverse classrooms: How to build on students' cultural strengths.* Alexandria, VA: ASCD.

Ungar, M. (2008). Putting resilience theory into action: Five principles for intervention. In L. Liebenberg & M . Ungar (Eds.), *Resilience in action* (pp. 17–38). Toronto, Canada: University of Toronto Press.

Werner, E., & Smith, R. S. (1992). *Overcoming the odds: High risk children from birth to adulthood.* Ithaca, NY: Cornell University Press.

Wolin, S., & Wolin, S. (1999). *Resilience as paradox.* Retrieved from http://projectresili-
    ence.com/resilience.htm

Contributors

Barbara Berté, JD, MPS, is a teacher of Social Studies at Archimedes Academy in New York City who earned her MPS degree in the School of Education at Manhattanville College, Purchase, New York. Her research examines the impact that warm demander pedagogy and the cultivation of meaningful and respectful relationships with students have on their academic success.

Frederick J. Brigham, PhD, is Associate Professor of Special Education at George Mason University in Fairfax, Virginia, and past president of the Council for Exceptional Children—Division for Research. Across his career, Dr. Brigham has served as a classroom teacher in elementary general education settings, a special education teacher in middle and high school settings, a program coordinator, and a director of special education.

Lou Denti, PhD, is the Lawton Love Distinguished Professor in Special Education at California State University, Monterey Bay, California. His research interests include classroom management, inclusion, secondary literacy, and social justice. His most recently published book is entitled *Proactive Classroom Management K-8: A Practical Guide to Empower Students and Teachers* (Corwin Press, 2012).

Maria G. Dove, EdD, is Associate Professor at Molloy College, Rockville Centre, New York. Previously, she taught ESL for over 30 years in K–12 and adult education programs in public and private school settings. Dr. Dove is the co-author of texts such as *Collaboration and Co-teaching: Strategies for English Learners* (2010) and *Common Core for the Not-So-Common Learn-*

er, Grades K-5: English Language Arts Strategies (2013) both published by Corwin Press.

Jeffrey P. Drake, PhD, an educational consultant, received his doctorate in curriculum and instruction from Kent State University in Kent, Ohio. He taught high school social studies and coached debate for 10 years before returning to the academy to study digital citizenship education. Dr. Drake served as District Coordinator for the Center for Civic Education's We the People curriculum and taught debate and instructional technology at The University of Findlay. His scholarship has appeared in the *International Journal of Instructional Technology* and the *Oregon Journal of the Social Studies.*

Jeanette L. Drake, PhD, is Associate Professor of Communication at The University of Findlay in Findlay, Ohio. With 15 years of traditional and online teaching experience at the undergraduate and graduate levels, her research interests include the intersection of online pedagogies, digital media, and public deliberation of social issues.

Martha Edelson, MA, is the Assistant Director for Curriculum and Teaching for Middle School at the Dalton School in New York City and Middle School Math Teacher. Prior to teaching at Dalton, Martha taught sixth-grade Language Arts and Social Studies at Little Red School House and Elisabeth Irwin High School for thirteen years. With over 25 years experience as an educator, she has worked as a consultant in the Norwalk, Connecticut, and Rancho Santa Fe public school systems and as a teacher trainer throughout Eastern Europe.

Ian M. Evans, PhD, is Professor Emeritus of Psychology at Massey University, Wellington, New Zealand, and a Fellow of the American Psychological Association. He is the co-author of *Warming the Emotional Climate of the Primary School Classroom* (2012, Dunmore Publishing, Auckland, New Zealand), and co-author, with Luanna Meyer, on two practical manuals for teachers and school leaders on restorative discipline.

Ryan Flessner, PhD, is Assistant Professor of Teacher Education at Butler University. Prior to that, he taught elementary school in Indianapolis and New York City. Dr. Flessner's interests include teacher research, early childhood and elementary education, and issues of equity, diversity, and social justice.

Anneli Frelin, PhD, is Assistant Professor in Curriculum Studies at the University of Gävle, Sweden with a background as a Middle school teacher.

She has published several books and articles, and her latest book is *Exploring Relational Professionalism in Schools* (Sense Publishers). She is presently involved in research on educational relationships in schools, teacher induction and a longitudinal study on teachers' commitment.

Vicky Giouroukakis, PhD, is Associate Professor in the Division of Education at Molloy College, Rockville Centre, New York. Her work has been featured in books and scholarly journals, and she frequently presents at regional, national, and international conferences. She is the co-author of *Getting to the Core of ELA, Grades 6-12: How to Meet the Common Core State Standards with Lessons from the Classroom* (2012) and *Getting to the Core of History/Social Studies, Science, and Technical Subjects, Grades 6-12* (2013), both published by Corwin.

Diane W. Gómez, PhD, is Associate Professor of Second Language Education and Chair of Educational Leadership and Special Subjects at Manhattanville College, Purchase, New York. This is her third chapter as co-author in the *Breaking the Mold* series. Her most recent book, *Changing Suburbs, Changing Students* (Corwin, 2012), is a collaborative work of the Changing Suburbs Institute®.

Bryan Harris, MEd, is the Director of Professional Development and Public Relations for the Casa Grande (Arizona) Elementary School District. He is the author of *Battling Boredom* (Eye On Education, 2010) and the co-author of 75 Quick and Easy Solutions to Common Classroom Disruptions (Eye On Education, 2012). His workshops, seminars, and publications focus on helping educators engage students and manage learning for student success.

Brittany L. Hott, PhD, is Assistant Professor of Special Education at Texas A&M in Commerce, Texas. Dr. Hott teaches research methods and psycho-educational assessment courses. Her research interests include emotional and behavioral disorders and academic interventions for secondary students with, or at risk for, emotional and behavioral disabilities.

Marcia B. Imbeau, PhD, is Professor of Curriculum and Instruction at the University of Arkansas working in the Childhood Education and Special Education programs preparing teachers to work in elementary classrooms and in gifted education programs. She is the co-author (with Carol Ann Tomlinson) of *Leading and Managing a Differentiated Classroom* (ASCD, 2010) and *Managing a Differentiated Classroom Grades K-8* (Scholastic, 2011). She is currently working to assist teachers with implementing the new *Common Core State Standards* utilizing quality curriculum design and differentiation and hopes this work will result in future publication

Howard M. Knoff, PhD, is the Director of Project ACHIEVE, an evidence-based school improvement program, and of the State Improvement Grant for the Arkansas Department of Education since 2003. Howie has authored 18 books, most recently *School Discipline, Classroom Management, and Student Self-Management: A Positive Behavioral Support Implementation Guide* with Corwin Press. A past-president of the National Association of School Psychologists, he is well known for his work in school improvement, school discipline/PBIS, behavioral interventions with challenging students, and multi-tiered Response-to-Intervention approaches.

Lori Langer de Ramirez, EdD, began her career as a teacher of Spanish, French, and ESL. She is currently the Director of World and Classical Languages & Global Language Initiatives at the Dalton School in New York City. Lori is the author of several books, including *Empower English Language Learners with Tools from the Web* and *Take Action: Lesson Plans for the Multicultural Classroom*, as well as several Spanish-language books and texts. Her website (www.miscositas.com) offers free materials for teaching Chinese, English, French, and Spanish.

Jennifer Lauria, EdD, is Associate Professor of Education and Director of Undergraduate Education Programs at Wagner College in New York City. Her areas of research include effects of learning-style responsive pedagogy and differentiated instruction, methods for incorporating educational technologies to enhance the teaching-learning process, meaningful collaboration in online learning communities, and the effects of health and wellness on teacher efficacy and learning outcomes.

Bettina L. Love, PhD, is Assistant Professor of Educational Theory and Practice at the University of Georgia. Her research focuses on the ways in which urban youth negotiate hip hop music and culture to form social, cultural and political identities. A continuing thread of her scholarship involves exploring new ways of thinking about urban education and culturally relevant pedagogical approaches for urban learners. She is the author of *Hip Hop's Li'l Sistas Speak: Negotiating Hip Hop Identities and Politics in the New South* (Peter Lang, 2012).

Micheline Susan Malow, PhD, is Associate Professor of Special Education at Manhattanville College in Purchase, New York. Her research has looked at adolescent risk taking behavior and teacher perceptions of classroom support. Her current research agenda includes strategies for working with at-risk students in school settings.

Hillary Merk, PhD, is Assistant Professor in the School of Education at the University of Portland, in Portland, Oregon. She received her PhD in education with an emphasis on classroom management and diversity, and a specialization in cultural studies and social thought in education from Washington State University in Pullman, Washington. Her research is focused in the areas of classroom management, diversity, and teacher education.

Luanna H. Meyer, PhD., is Professor Emerita at Victoria University of Wellington in New Zealand. She is first author of *The Teacher's Guide to Restorative Classroom Discipline* and *The School Leader's Guide to Restorative Classroom Discipline* both published by Corwin in 2012. She is also Editor for the discipline of Education of the Oxford Bibliographies Online (OBO) comprising up to date reviews published by Oxford University Press. Her current research addresses culturally responsive schooling and adolescent achievement motivation.

Jessica Minahan, MEd, BCBA, is a board certified behavior analyst and special educator. She is Director of Behavioral Services at NESCA-Newton (MA), as well as a school consultant to clients nationwide (www.jessicaminahan.com). She is the co-author of *The Behavior Code: A Practical Guide to Understanding and Teaching the Most Challenging Students* (Harvard Education Press, 2012).

Terry Murray, PhD, is Associate Professor in the Humanistic/Multicultural Education Program at SUNY New Paltz, New York. He is a former art teacher, YMCA professional, and trainer/consultant. His research interests focus on the interrelationship between knowledge, power, relationship, and place in teaching and learning, self-knowledge development, and contemplative education.

Jon Nordmeyer, MAT, is an instructional coach at the International School of Bangkok. He has been an educator for over 20 years, and has taught in international schools in The Netherlands, Turkey, Taiwan, and China. He has been a guest lecturer at the School for International Training, Harvard Graduate School of Education, and Tibet University. He has written for the *Journal of Staff Development and International Schools Journal.* He co-edited *Integrating Language and Content* (TESOL, 2010), shortlisted for the 2011 British Council ELTons Award for Innovation in English Teaching.

Marie Menna Pagliaro, PhD, is currently a professional development consultant. She was the Director of the Teacher Education Division at Dominican College, Chair of the Education Department at Marymount College, a student teaching supervisor at Lehman College, and science educator in the

Yonkers Public Schools, all in New York. Dr. Pagliaro is the author of six books, all published by Rowman and Littlefield. Among them are *Exemplary Classroom Questioning: Promoting Thinking and Learning* (2011); *Mastery Teaching Skills: A Resource for Implementing the Common Core State Standards* (2012); and *Academic Success: Applying Learning Theory in the Classroom* (2013).

Nancy Rappaport, MD, is Director of School Programs at the Cambridge Health Alliance and an associate professor of psychiatry at Harvard Medical School, Cambridge, Massachusetts (www.nancyrappaport.com). She is the co-author of *The Behavior Code: A Practical Guide to Understanding and Teaching the Most Challenging Students* (Harvard Education Press, 2012), and author of *In Her Wake: A Child Psychiatrist Explores the Mystery of Her Mother's Suicide* (Basic Books, 2009).

Carrie Rothstein-Fisch, PhD, is Professor of Educational Psychology and counseling at California State University, Northridge. She is a core researcher on the Bridging Cultures Project, a longitudinal action research project that employs a framework for understanding how teachers' culturally driven—and often unconsciously held—values influence classroom practice and expectations. She is author or co-author of six books and numerous articles on the topic of culture and education, including *Managing Diverse Classrooms: How to Build on Students' Cultural Strengths* (Rothstein-Fisch & Trumbull, 2008).

Karen Siris, EdD, is Principal of WS Boardman Elementary School in Oceanside, New York, and Adjunct Professor in the Educational Leadership program at Adelphi University in Garden City, New York. She is a member of the New York State Education Department's *Dignity Act Task Force,* a group planning the implementation of the New York State anti-bullying and harassment law. She is the co-author of *Stand Up!* (Createspace, 2012), a children's picture book on creating a *caring majority.* Her research on alleviating bullying won the H. Alan Robinson Outstanding Doctoral Dissertation Award from Hofstra University (2001).

Peter Stelzer, MA, JD, is a social studies instructor at Shanghai American School. Prior to his transition into education he was a practicing attorney for 12 years in the United States, focusing on litigation and criminal defense. He also led the Public Defender Office in Yap, Micronesia, and was the Legal Director in Beijing, China, for International Bridges to Justice, a human rights advocacy and education organization. He has been a presenter at legal and education training conferences throughout the United States, Asia and the Pacific.

Carol Ann Tomlinson, EdD, is the William Clay Parrish Jr. Professor and Chair of Leadership, Foundations, and Policy at Curry School of Education, University of Virginia. Prior to joining the faculty at the University of Virginia, she was a public school teacher in a differentiated classroom for 20 years. She is the author of over 250 articles and book chapters and ten books on differentiation including *How to Differentiate Instruction in Mixed Ability Classrooms* and co-author of *Differentiation and the Brain: How Neuroscience Supports the Learner-Friendly Classroom.* Her books have been translated into 13 languages.

Elise Trumbull, PhD, is an applied linguist and an educational consultant specializing in relations among language, culture, learning, and schooling. A former teacher and assessment coordinator for a K–3 public school, Dr. Trumbull has also taught college courses on language development and cognition. She has conducted research in cultural settings ranging from California, Washington, Florida, New York, and Arizona to various entities in Micronesia. Dr. Trumbull has co-authored dozens of articles and book chapters, as well as seven books.

Jennifer D. Walker, PhD, is Adjunct Instructor at George Mason University in Fairfax, Virginia. Dr. Walker has taught Secondary Curriculum and Strategies for Students with Disabilities, Behavior Management, and Characteristics of Exceptional Learners. Her research interests include emotional and behavioral disorders, tiered interventions, and team decision-making.

CPSIA information can be obtained at www.ICGtesting.com
Printed in the USA
BVOW08s0513031213

337950BV00001B/5/P